Chapters

Chapters

Demetri Barnes

Contents

1

∽

CHAPTERS

Hello everyone, welcome to chapters, my name is pen_to_brush.

This book is a consolidation of my writing spanning the years starting March 7 2016. I hope you all enjoy the journey from my mind and into my soul.

Hey you, yes you, the red pen lover, I hope you have fun reading, editing and correcting my book as well.

I write to inspire others, to give them freedom from their lives for just a moment, I write things that people can relate to...

I don't fancy myself a writer, I am more like a composer, my writing is like a symphony to me, each line is a different instrument, put together to come off as something classical and enlightening, freeing the mind, allowing it to soar like a bird brushing against the clouds.

Writers Note

In this book you will find desire, fire and pain possibly yourself. No, I'm not trying to drive you crazy, I'm trying to drive you to be the crazy woman you want to be in the bedroom, and set you free from that cage you've been keeping yourself in. Crazy is only a feeling that one has to feel to appreciate the calm after the storm of one finding herself. When i touch you, I won't only touch your body, but caress your soul, kiss you without laying my lips on you and make your heart pound without a touch. From one writer to my readers, you have started a fresh chapter in my book, that forces my hand to meet pen and put it to paper, to express new ways and byways to only get back to you. You my reader, enlightened, daring and waiting to receive your next message. I have no intentions on hurting you, but only want to see you happy, happy and free to be yourself within this moment of your life.

Chapter 1

Whispers into the Night

Feel me, Feel you

As I close my eyes and everything fades to black, I feel you in my arms. Listening to your heartbeat, feeling the rhythm of my heart compared to yours as I hold you close, and your body relaxes. I feel your heart as it slows to match mine. As our hearts beat as one, hand in hand, arm over arm I hold you close. as you lay in my arms it feels like time stops slightly just to share the moment. Being free, as our souls intertwine, energy fills the room, and our love bonds us more and more. The feeling of completeness, unconditional freedom to feel aware and alive, knowing no matter what I say no matter how strange it sounds I know that you'll understand. However, in this moment of silence no words are needed, we both can feel what the other feels, needs, or wants. You're my equal, my perfect imperfection, my missing puzzle piece.

Taste Me

Open your mouth and let me in. How do I taste? Do I melt in your mouth? OR do I make you melt from being in your mouth? Close your eyes, let your senses take life, mmmm how does it feel? Does it make your mind wonder? Does it make you long for more? As I go down do you feel me? Do I satisfy you as I go down inch by inch? Do you want more? Relax, enjoy the moment as I fill you up with my hardness and take a nibble. Who would have known a little bite would feel so good? As it gets deeper in you i watch you smile with delight, lick your lips, and end it with a simple bite of the lip...

My Lovelies

It's morning and all I can think about is my dick inside her. Stroke after stroke, fucking her softly and listening to her every breath. My hand on her shoulder, pulling her on to my dick, gliding deeper with every stroke. With my hand around her neck kissing her passionately caressing her beautiful breast as I fuck her harder and harder. Watching as she gets turned on by the sounds of her own moans. Pulling her closer as I bend you over her as she licks and sucks on your wet pussy dripping with every stroke of her tongue on your clit. Sliding in your ass as you push your hips up to me. Watching while you're fisting her pussy and sucking on her clit excites me. With every stroke getting harder and harder, swelling up in that ass waiting to bust. We change positions so I begin stroking my dick as y'all play, riding my face as you're having your way, grinding on my dick as I feel you both cum. Sucking my dick together waiting for my load, taking it deep down your perfect little throats the sweetest sounds of you gagging brings me closer. You're jacking it slowly and she's slowly licking the tip, kissing each other and put it between both of your lips. Not holding back much longer I reached my climax hearing you both moan with delight. Taking you both in my arms as you lay on my chest kissing you both on the forehead and whispering you're the best.

Submissive

Come in, sit down, I know what your body needs...

Sit there quietly you're going to learn your lesson indeed...

Close your eyes and my blade will satisfy my needs!!

Cutting away your top, layer by layer, until I start to see your lovely skin so soft and fair...

Open your mouth while I'm gripping her hair...

Sliding down her throat, throbbing and hard, you can hear her muffled moans out in the front yard...

Yanking her hair down making her drop to her knees, against the couch I thrust deeper with ease...

Picking her up and over the couch with ease, making that pussy drip with every tease, off ripped her panties from under her skirt, let's see how long I can tease before I make her squirt...

Smacking and squeezing her ass, making her work, if you cum before I tell you to there will be consequences, no dessert, no more play time you can only look...

to please master your will power is all that it took..

Opening that ass to take a lick, in her moan she asked daddy can I have your dick? With out thoughts or a shout, a quick yank to the head and gagged her mouth..

Taking her plug and aligning it in place sliding into her as I grab ahold of her waist. Listen to me I'm in control, learn your place!!

Toy after toy I'm filled with joy for she's such a good bad girl cuming with joy..

Daddy's little fuck toy, reminding her as I pound harder to fill her with joy.

Load after load is all she takes her screaming orgasms are the only things keeping her awake...

As my juices spill out of her, feeling it run over...

Don't mind the trail running down her legs, or the puddle leaking from the bed, tonight you're my toy to satisfy, and leave with a high. All that matters is the rope marks around your thighs... A memory that will remind you of tonight...

Lip Biter

Bite my lip as i grip your hair, with my left hand in the small of your back pulling you in closer, feeling your heartbeat against mine, breath for breath, feeling each other as one. Gripping your ass turning you against the wall pulling off your shirt, kissing the back of your neck, working my way down to the back of your shoulders, down your spine, unsnapping your bra, slowly caressing your soft skin, cupping your supple breasts. Slowly teasing your nipples as i kiss you from behind, then slowly caress your curves, down your sides, to your hips, gripping your yoga pants pulling them down, revealing more of your sexy flesh, spreading your legs apart, rubbing over your ass, around your hip, around to your inner thigh, feeling your juices drip on my finger tips (to be continued)

Thinking

Sitting here thinking about you, as I get weak. Thinking about the next time we'll be able to meet.

Touching your body just gives me a rise.

All I could think about was your thighs, and how they rise to bring me the prize within.

Kissing up your thighs slowly reaching my prize, slowly licking making your eyes roll back.

Nice and juicy but not to phat, going in deeper while you arch your back.

Hmmm nice and sweet, with every suck and lick your legs get weak.

No way I can have too much of you, I crave you every day of the week.

Guilty Fingers

I knew from the moment I met you I had to have you, I had to feel you, I had to please you, I had to let that wildfire that burns within you free! I knew only I could control you, only I could control that fire that rages within! Looking in those lustful eyes that begged to be punished and I was ever so happy to oblige. But deep down I knew you weren't like the others, simple handcuff, chains, and blindfolded wouldn't suffice. No. No, you were different. You're special!! Graceful muse, the worlds very own masterpiece. I knew with you I had to take my time! Bring you ultimate pleasure through pain. Feeling my hand around your throat as your heartbeat speeds, up pinning you against the wall wrapping your legs around my hips, feeling that naughty little pussy get wetter with every stroke. Asking and waiting for permission to cum over this dick. As your legs shake releasing your throat telling you to cum as you squirt all over me. You lose consciousness forcing me to hold on to you until we reach the bed. Dropping you then tying you to the bed disappointed with your passing out. Wrapping twine around your beautiful supple breast and pulling it tight. As you awaken to the feel of the wand vibrating against your clit, I joyfully tease the big juicy nipples. Hearing your moans as I tease you, letting the climax build slowly, just as you get close, the wand turns off, then back on to watch it build again, cum for me you hear, as I slowly untie your breast. Telling you if you pass out again, you're not sleeping for the next two nights!! Understood? Yes, you screamed quickly, releasing your breast as you squirt across the room, soaking the bed as her body trembles. Reaching up wrapping my hand around your throat telling you to stay with me, never releasing the wand from your clit. Feeling your body shake, until your eyes start to roll to the back of your head. Releasing your throat and taking away the wand untying one of your legs and placing it on my shoulder as I slide deep into you, giving you every inch of me, fucking you like the sweet little whore you've always wanted to be.

Play for Keeps

Playing for keeps is putting everything out there, being the best, so they won't want to leave, nor think about being with someone else. If and anytime someone comes up against me, I always play for keeps. Have an open mind and do something the next man won't. If you do the same thing that the last man did, do it better! Put it down so good that she'll forget who did it first. If somehow you have a friend that is scared of commitment and would like to keep it sexual, play for keeps. Put it down as if your life depends on it and they'll forget about their fear. The most important thing about playing for keeps is knowing how to manage an orgasm, if you cum to quick it could be over, or if you let them reach their climax before you're ready to cum they might call in a rain check, depending on how big the orgasm was. Now controlling the orgasm is about knowing the person you're with, how they body react to a touch, lick, or the slightest breath. In theory all orgasm are mental, so if the person you're with feels safe with you and know they have security with you they will let go and have bigger orgasms. Building an orgasm consist of knowing the person you're with like I said before as you play talk to her, keep her focus on you, when you start to feel her tighten up STOP wait a couple seconds kiss her or caress her (whatever works for you) and slowly start back stroking if you still feel the orgasm there pull back without coming completely out and slowly stroke with the head, by this time she would want it more if you must change positions just to keep her from reaching her climax. Make sure it's a position where you can control the strokes DO NOT LET HER RIDE. So, by this time the orgasm went down start back but start deep, if it from the back beat it. Carful not to cum wile you're doing this. But wait until you start to feel it to build again slow town and talk to her that will get her mind off the orgasm wile you slow stroke it, for the last time when you feel it start to build again beat it, until she explode don't stop, at the same time as she do open her legs and rub her clit to keep the orgasm going until your back hard or she can't take it anymore if you didn't go down while you reached your climax stick it back in and keep her stimulated until you or her can't go anymore..

Damn I wish it was real!

Sitting here in the rain thinking about my love and its pain. Wishing the rain could wash away the flames from my passion burning of what we can and will be. Burning, from the passion of every touch, caress, and kiss. Your touch, like heaven, soft, caring, and so much love as you rub up and down my body, stroking my dick with every turn. Damn. I wish it was real. Caressing my head slowly, jacking, teasing the tip of my dick damn. I wish it was real. Kissing you softly, putting all my passion into every kiss placed softly on your body. Caressing your every curve, feeling your passion build with every inch of me in you lol damn. I wish it was real. The thoughts of us getting married, building our foundation, as a family growing, loving and learning from each other fulfilling each other wildest dreams. DAMN I WISH IT WAS REAL

Lies and Secrets

Seeing your beautiful face staring into your eyes as you smile at me, as I'm smiling at you innocently, but deep down inside secretly knowing the things I want to do to you. Watching you as you walk by not know how much I want to bend you over the table and violate you in the best ways possible, to hear you moan as you grip the tablecloth from my tongue stroking your clit from the back, gripping your ass while my tongue slides in and out of you revealing your perfect little opening. Growing throbbing getting harder waiting and wanting to slide in you. With both hands spreading your plump ass apart sliding my tongue up and down across your hole while my two fingers slide in and out of your sweet little pussy, stroking more and more with my tongue the wetter I feel you get with your juices dripping from cumin over my fingertips with my tongue in your ass, feeling your body quiver with every stroke of my tongue pushing you to pure ecstasy. Unbuttoning my pants letting them fall around my ankles as my hard dick throbs, while sliding in your perfect little hole, as you grip the edges of the table bitting the table cloth trying not to scream and give away our location. Gripping your hips pulling you closer to me as the final inch slide in you as you raise to your tip toes with delight.

Watching you prance around the house with barely anything on excites me to no end. Round ass, perfectly round juicy nipples, teasingly saying my name, resisting my urge to take you right here and now. Watching you walk by as your hips sway side to side with out you noticing, waiting for the moment I can make you mine, your teasing has gone on for too long.

Another again until the end.

The Sun is rising, glistening through the blinds, shining against your skin as it glows with warmth as you lay in my arms with your head in my chest as my finger tip slowly runs up and down your spine, lightly careful not to wake you. As I lay here on my back, I am thinking back over the night and where it started. Saturday morning, just out of the shower, early morning phone call. Typical Saturday, my usual on call phone calls, I pack up my table, supplies, then get dressed so I can start the day. I load up the truck and as I go to pull out the driveway I see you passing, not thinking anything of it I continue to pull out. As the day goes on, five massages down, I head out for lunch thinking back to you. I try to shake those thoughts as I drive to Jimmy John's for my favorite sandwich. as I sit down to eat, I receive a text saying, "how's your day going daddy?" "good" I responded, "by the way who's this?" I take my fist bite and wait for a response thinking this must be a wrong number. As I finish my lunch, my alarm goes off reminding me I have a meeting in 45 minutes. I pack up my trash to toss out, i start out the door and I hear "sir, you forgot your key" as she walks over to me, I look down in my hand at my keys, smile and reply "sorry I have my keys here." I look up and I noticed something familiar about the key she was handing me. It is the key that I had made for her. I take the key as a tear runs down my face. As I get in the truck, I placed the key in my cup holder. I sit and stare in the mirror as memories flash through my mind. Suddenly my thoughts are interrupted by a text saying "you'll find out tonight.' I didn't think anything of it, I was still convinced it was the wrong number. After the meeting is over, I head home, pulling into the garage I noticed a single rose petal with shades of white and pink, with a slight red tip. The petal causes an alarm to go off in my head. I round my truck trying to see if anyone was there. I don't have a rose bush, neither do any of my neighbors. standing at the edge of the driveway thinking how strange this day is becoming, the wind blows as i raise my hand and open it letting the petal float away in the breeze. I unlock the door and walk in the house, to my bedroom I go, turning on the shower, I undress and step into the shower under the hot water, just letting it beat against my skin, thinking about you, the last time I saw you. You smiled and walked out of my life and on to the new job offer. I get out of the shower, dry off, and contemplate what to wear out tonight. My mind tells me it's a beautiful so all black makes the most sense. I drove across the city and pulled up to a bar with the music blasting. I walk in, shake hands with security as everyone greets me. One face sticks out of the crowd more than the others, I looked into her eyes as she got closer. I could smell the sweet fragrance of her perfume. As I got closer time stopped and the music dampened. Flash backs started to play in my head, remembering her soft skin, and the feel of her lips. Pulling her from the bar stool holding her in my arms with a warm embrace. "I've missed you so much" we whispered in each other's ears. We leave the bar and head to the beach, hand in hand we walk under the night sky, who knows how much time has passed by. Catching up as the night gets deep. We head back to my place while I'm thinking oh my god I can't wait. We pull into the driveway, I walked around to open her door, then I remember the last time her clothes hit my floor. Time ticks down as she lays closer to me and places her head on my chest, I kiss her on the forehead and said "I love you" holding her through the night wishing the moment would never end. Now the sun is rising, glistening through the blinds, shining against your skin as it glows with warmth as you lay in my arms with your head in my chest as my fingertip slowly run up and down your spine, lightly careful not to wake you. As I lay here on my back, I am thinking back over the night and where it starts and how it ended. A love so deep came to an end I lost you my lover and my best friend. But in the end you came home to rest until our souls meet again...

SHE

She might be you; she could be you; she could be the one that I mistake you for in the midnight hour.... She

She... She could be the one that I have wake-less dreams about, that my body longs for that causes me to toss and turn from missing her... She

She.... She could be my dreams, my universe, the one that brightens my day, maybe she is you, maybe she isn't you maybe she..... She...

She is my lover in the freakiest night, my porn star in the latest hour, the one that can take my breath away she is....

She... She is or could be the one that I fall asleep to, and the first beautiful smile I see each morning, she ...... She is... She isn't... Maybe she isn't real, maybe she, she may not be the girl next door, the girl that you may think she is, I don't know, she.... She is....

She is my wife, my lover, my best friend, she is my ex's combined into one, she is... She is the unlikely, the thoughts wrapped up in my twisted thoughts, she is....

She is the leading force that pumps my blood through my veins... She is....

She's my uncontrollable anger that burns passionately with in, my sense of calmness, she is the unstable balance within my balanced world she is... SHE...

Most Don't Know

Here's some things most males/females don't know.

1.) Orgasms are mental. yea yea the physical activity is good, but it's really not needed to do so. in the moment females are most likely to think themselves out of an orgasm. How? Deeply within the back of your mind it's something there that's blocking you from reaching that peak. Also, it could be a comfort issue, physically you may feel comfortable but something within may not be settled, in turn goes back to a mental issue. To fully ensure you reach your climax make sure you're comfortable, all things within yourself is settled, and you can enjoy the moment...

Lick

Lick by lick, stroke by stroke, deeper and deeper my tongue goes, in and out in deeper and out again as your orgasm began. Grab my head, clench the sheets, eat you until your knees get weak. The more I eat, the wetter the sheets, the more I eat the more you weep, pretty soon you'll be fast asleep, in dream land you will go, where I'll make love to you nice and slow.

Dream A Dream

From In the pool against the wall, to in the house against the door, as I peel your clothes off, pick you up and slide in you as you grind on while I carry you down the hall to the shower, kissing you softly feeling your wet body against mine skin to skin, as the water from the shower runs down our bodies, stroking you deep as your nails dig into my back pulling me closer. Looking in your eyes as I caress your body feeling your soft lips against mine drives me crazy. From the shower to the bed as I work my way down your body as you hold on to my head, between your breast, down past your belly button as your legs shake. The farther I get the more you shake, nibbling on your inner thigh, as you open up wider, spread your lips and latch on to your clit softly sucking as my tongue rolls against it, mmm roll your body to me, as you close your eyes and scream wile your body quake with every orgasm Turn over!! Smack that ass, mmmm want it deeper? Here!! As I grab ahold of your hair. Beep beep beep.. ohhhh what a dream

Time

Let time tick away...

Here in my arms where I watch you lay...

Tick to the tock.... tock to the tick..

Slowly kissing your body thinking of all the places I'm going to lick...

As I get harder from you caressing my dick...

Time ticks away as I slide in you mmmmm a perfect fit...

On and on you're riding it deep..

After our climax we're fast asleep...

In my arms there's no need to count sheep...

For in my arms close to my heart is where you'll always sleep..

My Woman like my Car

Ok gloves coming off with this one...

Women, sexy, tatted, best riders, smooth, candy paint, eye candy, power, swerving right to left, shifting gears, mmmmm damn..

I don't treat my woman like any other Nigga did or would. My woman is like my car. There's nothing like a car fresh off the lot, sexy, modified to your tuning, not to flashy, slide in, fitting you like a glove, listen and feeling her purr, there's nothing like putting the first mile on her in her shifting gears, as the wind smack her sexy ass.... Driving deep in and out, as she purrs with every press of the pedal, enjoying the power as I take control, sweating like being out in the sun on the beach, as the excitement and power makes my heart pound, living on the edge, closing my eyes at each orgasmic moment rushing in and through every vein in your body. There's nothing like the rush of building up to the moment where you feel like you're ready to explode as the hair raises from your body with excitement as you get closer and closer to the edge you're about to scream. Take a moment and appreciate her, fulfill her every demand, make her your number one, you wouldn't abuse your car so don't abuse her. This is my woman and my car...

Drive

Let's take a drive to an destination unknown, let's enjoy each other as the trip unfold, randomly pull over and put you on the hood of the car, undressing you as the rain drops splash off of your body, as the drops slide down your frame highlighting your soft sweet skin dripping off of your nipples, sliding down your body as I pull you closer, opening you up for a taste. As my head gets deeper and deeper between your thighs softly licking and sucking on your clit. Caressing your nipples as you try to catch your breath, wrapping your legs around my head as you reach your climax. As the cold rain rub against your hot body it shakes with every drop, lifting your legs to my shoulders grabbing ahold of your juicy, moist, hips as I slide in, felling your every pulse, with every stroke, your every breath with every caress...

Word Play

This is my day to do a word play. No censers, or crowd control you just getting me total package and oh so bold, like the freak in me worth more then gold. In my hand my dick i hold hard and throbbing, standing there like a pole. Bend over and let me slide in, slow poking and stroking i work just like a pen. Wile i slide in and out caressing each curve smacking that ass cause i have much nerve! Unlike most men i take my time and i love to hit that spot time after time. So warm and dripping wet Damn ma we going to need a new sheet sets. Lets change the position and yet i have to mention, i've been waiting to taste you all night so grab the sheet it's no need to fight, as my tongue flick up and down on your clit your body shiver with every lick, For ever pleased for eternity as time tick, . This is my word play I'm out of time catch me next time and i'll tell you the rest of this rhyme.

Word Play 2

Laying here alone, listing to music on my phone, thinking about hearing you moan, as we make love to this song all night long. Who would have thought something so good could be so wrong. Nothing sweeter than the tone of your voice as you moan, as we rollover hold on tight because it's going to be a long night. Don't be scared no worries no need to fright I'll be gentle while I work it right. Hold on to the pillow and take a bite, while I beat it how you like. Deeper and deeper I'll go, work that body to the flow. On and on the song flow, as you pull me close and whisper more. To sleep we both go, laying in each other's arms, don't worry about the air, I'll keep you warm...

Saturday Night

The night is long, the moon is full, and love is lingering through the night air. My arms are open to letting love in, as it knocks on my front door. Wearing that black dress that I love so much, caressing her every curve, high lighting every detail of her sexy figure. As my mind wonders what's underneath, slow music plays, bringing out dinner with no delay, next round is R Kelly's 12 play!! uummm strawberries, with whip cream, as you lay in my lap, gentle kisses and caresses, are the best to set this mood. As you lay there as I gaze in your eyes hearing whispers of I love you as they float from your lips. as we move from the living room to the bed, you sit me on the bed and say "daddy I have a surprise for you", as you slip on some music and start to dance slowly for me, teasing me with every stroke of your hips, slowly revealing this lacy, sexy, pink and black teddy. slowly unwrapping like a piece of candy, so tempted to taste in every way as you tell me to relax baby, this is my time to please you. Slowly laying me down, undressing me, as you stroke my hard but waiting dick, as it pulses for you over and over, as you drop to your knees as my pants drop to the floor taking me in your mouth. Teasing the head nice and slow stroking ...

Another Random

It's nothing sexier then a thick woman that carry her self the way a real woman should. Give my mind something to wonder about. Let me try to figure out what's on under that top, that hold your full breast up at attention. Just asking to be licked, or how you got into those pants that look like they were painted on, That caress your hips that hold on to that ass like my hands with glue on them. Don't make it so easy for me this bull love to chase lol run in circles with my tongue out like a kid in a candy store. Hips and thighs always so warm keeping that fruit nice and ripe just waiting to be tasted, juicy. Women are one of a kind no two are made alike. Unlike fruit they may look alike but no two taste the same, some are bigger than others, some may even squirt when you bite into it. Most men wouldn't admit it, but women really do make the world go round.

Love Afire

In times of darkness the truth will bring you light. If you seek the light seek the one who provides it for you to see..

"Come in, and close the door, cut off your phone. Get undressed, come here" she said "I've been waiting on you." "Wait," he said "what about your husband?" She smiled, "Oh he's working late and so are you." As they laughed, he asked her , "Why? why cheat, does he not treat you right?" She looked him in the eyes "No, that's not it. I'm happy he treats me like a queen, I just want you." "Mmmm" he said, as she got on her knees, she slurped on his dick taking it deeper and deeper as he leaned his head back, and asked her "Are you sure you want to do this?" She replied "ssshhh come give me that dick!!" Pulling him down on top of her. As he entered her slowly, stroking over and over as she screamed with delight. The moment I entered the house I heard them. So, I walked through the house, past the kitchen, down the hall to the gun case. I reached for my 9 & two clips. The shot gun she bought me with its engraved LOVE FOR-EVER. Clinching it tighter and tighter as I loaded each slug. I chocked it while walking to my bedroom. Suddenly he stopped and whispered "shh!! what was that?" as he listened, she said, "nothing" and turned over for him as he slid his dick back in her from the back. Doggy style as she likes it. I closed my eyes not thinking clearly. Thinking about the moments we shared as I made my way upstairs, down the hall, cutting through the bathroom entering the room and pressing the end of my cold steel barrel against his bald head. He went limp, she turned to look back at him and she faced the barrel of my 9. Damn. As I repeated the questions, calmly, from before they started. Demanding an answer, he tried to speak until he felt a nudge from the shot gun, "Not you! I want her answer!" She was clearly in shock as the words fumbled from her mouth. "I, I, I thought you were on a business trip." My anger was boiling "Answer me!!! Why? Why not just leave?" As the tears rolled down her face, she yelled "I don't know!" That answer aggravated me even more. "Don't lie to me!" I moved my finger closer to the trigger narrowing down my aim. "Wait!" yelled the guy. I glance down at him, and I asked "What?" He mumbled "I asked the same thing." As if somehow, that made it all ok. "But it didn't stop you, did it?" As I slammed him in the head with the butt of the shot gun he fell over and she went to catch him. "Don't move!" I yelled. "Why?!" I asked holstering my 9. She was now facing my shot gun. "Why?"she explained that she has been seeing him for years. As I started to squeeze the trigger. Buzz buzz buzz my alarm goes off... Lol ahh just a dream...

Welcome Home

Dick hard, swollen, throbbing, pulsating waiting on you to come home. Slowly rubbing the head of my dick as you walk through the door smiling, dropping everything at the door, I begin unwrapping you piece by piece. No shirt, no panties, no bra, just your skirt and heels, grabbing that ass pinning you against the wall, kissing down your body putting your legs over my shoulders as is stand back up as you slide up the wall. Lick, lick, slurp, your juices run down my face, you grab my head while

I'm licking your clit, feeling your body tremble, over to the couch bending you over the arm, sliding in slowly, inch by inch, teasing your pussy as you anxiously wait for me to hit that spot. "Fuck me daddy" I hear you moan, ramming my dick in you feeling you getting wetter with every stroke, holding on to the back of your skirt tightly yanking you back harder on this dick, feeling your juices drip down my balls smacking that pussy with every stroke. On to the bed as you lay me on my back, taking my dick into your mouth, teasing the head with your tongue, grabbing your hair as you're taking it deep, swallowing my dick as I fuck your face waiting for a climax. Ride me baby I mumbled harder than ever, you're so sexy crawling up the bed, holding on to your ass, as you ride me slow, taking it deeper and deeper the harder you go. You're grinding on the dick nice and slow, taking your breast in my mouth, teasing, licking, and sucking. You're taking it faster and faster, as I get harder and harder. "Fill me up daddy!" as I explode, grinding again as you reach your climax, taking in every drop from my dick. As you lay on top of me tired from work, I hold you closely and asked you about your day..

Exchange

I can't help but to feel the need to deny myself the simple pleasures and feeling the need to completely indulge myself into the more complex joy. All while fulfilling the task of pleasing you higher than the pleasure you received last time we touched. I can't help but please you. I cherish your nails in my back, bites around my neck and chest, in return to your punishment, you get pent down and fucked until you can't cum anymore, equally bitten, pussy drilled, sore legs, but the most fulfilling smile the next morning when you awake and see my face. You're my punisher and I'm your master...

Good Girl

"Come here, take them off and give them to me!" "Yes sir" she replies. Mmmm yes, gripping her ass, picking her up, and sitting her on the table. Clenching her hair in my fist, kissing her slowly, feeling her hands rubbing the front of my pants asking, "Can I have it daddy?" With pleasure I say, "Yes baby girl take what's yours." She unties my sweats and slides her hand down to pull it out. It throbs in her hands, as she wraps her legs around me, I kiss around her neck and shoulders. Feeling her hot juicy pussy as she slides me in her. I lay her back, pulling her to the edge of the table, so that her ass is hanging slightly off the table. I place her legs on my shoulders as I slide in deeper. Hearing her moan makes me harder, makes me want her more, makes me fuck her harder. We have done this many times before, but this time it was different, we recently discovered a different part of our relationship, and made her submission official. Taking her legs from my shoulders, taking her and bending her over the table, slide in her, gripping her hips, gave her all of me, over and over again, filling her with every drop. Turning her back around, I could see the proud look on her face, knowing she was Daddy's Good Girl

Slave

Come here. Lay down. I tie you to the bed. Tonight, you're my slave. Blind fold on, silence. I tear your shirt open. Rip your skirt off. I begin by teasing your nipples with my tongue. Now taking an ice cube and letting the water drip down the center of your chest. Teasing your nipples with the ice cube as they get harder. Now taking it in my mouth. Melting it as you moan. Dripping the water from the ice cube down your body as my mouth follows. Taking the ice cube in my mouth again. Kissing your pussy lips before I open them. Slowly licking your clit. Stimulating your pussy like never before. Licking slow enough to get you close to your climax but not letting you release. Listening to you begging for more as I tease your pussy. My dick gets harder and harder. Untying one of your legs, putting it on my shoulder as I slide in you. Feeling you melt as your legs tremble with pleasure. Slowly stroking your pussy waiting for your climax to build. Feeling your pussy squeeze around my dick I pull out and smack that pussy as you beg me to let you cum. Untying your other leg, I slide back in you. Deeper and deeper until I'm balls deep inside of you. Stroking, hitting that same spot with my hand around your throat. Telling you to cum, while I pound that pussy. As you reach your climax, screaming, I hold my dick deep in you, feeling your body shake as you squirt all over me. Turning you over. Smacking that ass. While you scream "Yes daddy give it to me!" Sliding in you from the back feeling your juices drip from my dick. Feeling that ass bounce up and down. Pounding that pussy as I start to reach my climax, I hold on to your hips pulling you back on my dick making sure I give you every drop of my cum. Untying your hands, you lay me down and start to suck and slurping on my dick as you stroke it with your hand. Looking up at me asking "Who's your little slut?" The sweetest satisfaction fills me as I respond "You are, my queen." You respond "good." coming back up to lay on my chest.

Whispers into the Night

It's the moments when you can't sleep, and she's talked to you until she has fallen asleep. And it's quiet, you're lying in the dark, that's when you miss her the most. The feel of her skin, pressed up against yours, your hand cupping her breast, and you're kissing the back of her neck. Your dick between her legs, while she grinds on it in her half sleep state. Your hand slowly sliding down her side getting to that favorite part of her hip where your hand fit perfectly, you grip it, and she moans. Rolling her hip back so your dick can slide deep rubbing against her now dripping pussy. It's moments like this that I live for, but it's the moments we're apart that makes me want her more and count down the hours to when she'll return to my bed, to my arms, she returns to her man, to his kisses, to his soft touches that she once hated but now drives her wild.

Fuck Me

Stimulate my mind, get my blood racing, rub my dick through my pants.. I want you to fuck me..

Take off your shirt, tie me to the bed, tease my lips with your nipples. Fuck me.

Slowly stroke my head, then down my shaft, teasing my dick as I throb in your hand..mmmm fuck me..

Sliding me in and out of your mouth, fast and then slow making my nut build up then stopping. Please fuck me.

Taking my dick sliding my head in and out as slow as you can, once down my shaft feeling your juices.. Oh my god fuck me..

Slide down me taking me deep, grinding, circling, and bouncing. Fuck uhh yes fuck me.

Sinking your nails in my chest, as you cum harder then ever with excitement.

Ahh fuck me..

Speed up, take it deep, feel me as I reach my climax, moaning to you yes fuck me, just as I start to let go, you grab my face demanding me to wait. Going down to put me back in your mouth taking me deep until I can't hold it any more, releasing as I feel you take me down your throat, sucking up every drop.

Slow Dance

Let's set the mood, there's a room full of couples, slow dancing, the lights are low, and the song I want to be your man is playing softly in the background. And across the room comes walking in, Her! Her beauty shines from across the room, and your heart feels like it's trying to jump out of your chest, across the room to join hers. As you get closer the song changes, Piece of my love starts playing, as your hands meet, grabbing her pulling her into your arms, and you smell her, she lays her head in your chest, and the room turns black. Everyone fades and there is no longer anyone there, but you and her, the warmth of her body and your heart starts to slow, and you feel the sync of you both becoming one in that moment. Then Ready or Not by After 7 comes on, you feel your hears beat as one quickly and you both quickly realize this is your moment, the night you've both been waiting for.

Finally, I have her, where she belongs, this is so perfect, she, she smells so good. The feel of her skin, she's so soft, feeling her body sway with mine as one, it feels like we're floating. Kissing her forehead I feel her grip my shirt, trying to get closer then she already is. Hoping the next song to play would be MY MY MY by Johnny Gill, and without a hint I hear it start to play, and all I can do is smile and start to hum to her, as my hands slide down her back, to the small of her back. Tonight, I'm going to make my intention clear. After that song goes off, I feel her pull away, and grab my hand, and start to walk, so I follow, down the hall, the further we get the more and more the music fades. Rounding the corner, I pull her close to me, and kiss her, slowly pinning her to the wall, with her hands above her head, letting go I feel her hands caress my face, and I hear her say softly while she kisses me, "Let's get out of here. " "Let's." I agree. The ride home was incredible, we laughed, talked, and talked about music. It couldn't have been more perfect. Approaching the house, pulling over to the curb, I turn the car off, get out and walk around to open her car door to let her out and to walk her to the door. Approaching the door, I wrap her up in my arms as if this will be the last time, I'll ever see her again. "I enjoyed tonight.", I said as I released her from my arms, she kissed me softly and replied "So did I." She smiled, unlocked the door, then entered the house. "Good night gorgeous!" Walking back to the car, I can't help but to smile, getting back into the car, pulling away from the curb, I drive around the corner and enter into the garage, lock up, and make my way into the house. Starting from the front door, there's a trail of rose peddles, and her clothes. Following her trail, to the bathroom, dropping my last piece of clothing as I enter the shower, there she was, waiting as the water ran down her body, the lights flicker off of her body, taking her hips into my hands, kiss her softly around the back of her neck, I reach around her and side my fingers between her legs, I hear her gasp, her hand rubbing through my head, tuning off the water, I pick her up and carry her to the bed, lay her down and kiss her, working my was down her body, stopping at her breasts, take my time and tease her nipples before moving down lower, over her hips, down over the outside of her thighs and back up between her inner thighs, kissing her lips, as they open slowly as I grip her thighs, until her clit reaches my tongue, she grips the sheets, and I softly suck her clit, a night of pleasure is ahead of us both..

Tonights Fun

Tonight, you watch, you can't touch, only thing you get to do is sit here, cuffed to this chair with this bag in your mouth. We can only touch you, tease you, lick you, suck you.

Sitting here watching them kiss, hearing them moan as they lick each other's breasts fingering each other looking at me as I get harder as my dick throb with every waiting moment as the reach they're climax.. As my wife squirt from her friend fisting.. Watching her pussy drip, glisten, as she shake with pleasure.. As her friend walks over to me and grab me by my hair slowly grinding on my dick. I hope to slip in, if only for a moment. Feeling her wet pussy rub over my dick is driving me crazy, as my wife crawls over from the bed. I can feel her tongue lick the other side of my dick as I start to throb faster and harder with excitement, coming closer to my climax. Her friend gets up and takes my wife by her shoulders, turns her around and sits her on my lap. I can feel her pussy graze over my dick as her lips wrap around it. Her friend puts on a strap on. Waiting to see what happens, I briefly get distracted by my wife's pussy getting wetter and starting to pulse as she gets excited. Walking back over to my wife, opening her mouth, pushing the dildo in deep making her gag. I get to feel her squirm in my lap as she gets wetter. "Come here, bend over, yeah, put your mouth right there, suck his dick. Yea like that spread your legs, yea let me slide in that tight little pussy, you like that?"

Feeling her in my tight pussy felt so good, ramming me deeper and deeper, grabbing my husband thighs tighter and tighter, feeling him get harder in my mouth knowing he's going to unload a sweet treat in my mouth. Taking him deeper, waiting to take every drop, "Oh God! I'm cumin! Yes! More please yes yes!" "Oh you like that huh?

Now turn your sweet ass around and slide that gorgeous dick in and ride him like your life depends on it!" Feeling my wife slide me in her ass felt better than ever. Her friend reclines my chair I can feel myself getting deeper in her ass with every inch that I lay back. Feeling my wife hug my dick as every inch of me slides in. I can feel her loosen up as she gets past the pain and starts to enjoy it. Feeling her start to speed up, going up and down bouncing on my dick as her friend eats her pussy. Her friend stands up and lays my wife back over me. I'm still deep in my wife as her friend slides in her pussy with the strap on. I feel it get tighter as my wife moans from the double penetration. As we enter my wife, I can feel her gripping the handles of the chair shaking as she climaxes.

I never knew I could feel such pleasure from having both of my holes filled, wrapping my legs around Angela as I climax feeling my husband dick so deep in my ass throbbing as his cum spills out. "Baby do you want me to let you lose?? Does my good boy want to play?" We both laugh as we uncuffed him from the chair. "Mmmmmmm finally." he said taking me and Angela to the bed..

Mental Stimulation

Mentally stimulate me, tease me, make me laugh, give me something to think about, lead me to variables of conclusion that forces me to define the difference from favorable outcomes. Take my mind and run with it, stimulate me to a point that the thought of you makes me drool. Stimulation. Give it to me take me to that edge and kick me off, stimulate me the break of a full-on mental climax, calm me down, work me back up and shock me then push me back down, climb on top of me slowly grind me, rub your fingers over my head tease me, hop up, deny me pleasure, until I rip your clothes off. Stimulate me...

I want to be the reason you're wet

Yeah girl!! That's it Check yourself out

Fuck yeah turn that ass around, take a look, take a pic, put that ass in my hands, is that what you need help with?

Oh, let's make this a better trip

Bend you over, press that button

Open your mouth, swallow this dick.

Skirt up, legs sped fingers in that pussy

Ass smacking, throat fucking, & finger fucking that pussy

Dick hard, throbbing, panties ripped and pulled off to the side

Up against the wall with your legs on my shoulders, slamming you on this dick with every thrust

Yelling and screaming is a must

Hold on to that bar, and your leg right there

Fucking that pussy while pulling her hair, no you can't cum yet, no you better not dare!!! Grabbing her by the throat, now look into my eyes, now slide this dick back inside

Moaning wildly, grinding, with her nails in my back, screaming daddy please

Yes my love as she let go, juices drip down my dick, to my balls

Feeling her tremble, with such delight I couldn't help but to take a bite, unloading into her as she cum again all over my pipe

Down to her knees, to finish the job, before she knew it she was turned around

Legs wrapped around my head; I feel her taking my tongue deep as if she was being fed

This will be continued until we get to bed

Swimming Pool

From In the pool against the wall, to in the house against the door, as I peal your clothes off, pick you up and slide in you as you grind on me while we head down the hall. Down the hall to the shower, kissing you softly feeling your wet body against mine skin to skin, as the water from the shower runs down our bodies, stroking you deep as your nails in my back pulling me closer. Looking in your eyes as I caress your body feeling your soft lips against mine drives me crazy. From the shower to the bed as I work my way down your body as you hold on to my head, between your breast, down past your belly button as your legs shake.. The farther I get the more you shake, nibbling on your inner thigh, as you open up wider, spread your lips and latch on to your clit softly sucking as my tongue rolls against it, mmm roll your body to me, as you close your eyes and scream wile your body quake with every orgasm. Turn over!! Smack that all ass, mmmm want it deeper? Here!! As I grab ahold of your hair. Beep beep beep.. Uuuhh a dream

Office Party

It's new years, the company is having a party. Trisha the intern just arrived. She begins mingling through the room, while I'm standing by the bar watching her beauty shine. Just looking into her eyes I can see her innocence, but looking at her smile I can tell she is a bad girl just waiting to be set free. Her voice, refreshing like a summers rain after a year long drought. Hair flowing just waiting to blow in the much deserving wind. With a walk that can set the room on fire with every step. Properly speaking, as every tone dances its way to my heart, knocking heavily at my door of love. Seeing you, undressing you with my eyes, wanting to take you where you stand, taking you against the wall from behind, ripping your dress open and peeling it away from your beautiful skin.. "Omar" I hear a voice say. Looking up "Huh? Yea?" As she ask "How are you?" Answering slowly trying not to make a fool of my self as she congratulate me on the deal that was closed with our law firm. As she talked her words faded and all I could focus on was her mouth, as those beautiful full lips turn me on. ALL I could see was her saying *yes daddy fuck me!* Smiling I asked her to excuse me. Leaving the room to go to the bathroom excited close to my climax I had to finish it off with her in mind.. Closing the bathroom door with a quick click, I continued to unzip my pants as my dick fell out pulsating waiting to be touched.. Stroking my dick leaning against the wall excited about to climax and out the corner of my eyes I noticed another door, cracked... Slowly moving with dick in hand quietly trying to reach the door with out making a sound. Reaching the door still hard as a rock, there she was undressing, thinking please don't turn around, but thinking this is my lucky day. Not knowing that she had seen me already, I heard her voice say "Don't just stand there come in." I quickly tried to put my dick away when she said "Don't bother." walking into the room she sat down on the bed. Waiting to take a taste, teasing me at first with her tongue on the top of my dick taking it slowly in and out of her mouth. Grabbing her hair as I fucked her face, as she take me deeper as I climax careful not to waste a drop.

Saharan Fire Ball

It's the little things about her that turns me on, the way she licks the tip of her finger, then rubs the tip of my dick until it starts to get hard, while she looks me in my eyes. Then bringing that finger back up to her mouth so she can taste me without breaking eye contact. How she sits on my lap quietly as I tie her breast together, meanwhile getting wetter and wetter from feeling me throbbing inside her, fighting the urge to move, because she was told to sit still. Or when she's being my muse, standing still, as I slowly walk around her, slowly undressing her, kissing her body as each piece of clothing reveals more of her beautiful soft skin, as they drop to the floor, teasing her clit with my finger tip, while gripping her hair. The sounds of her moans echoes through the room. Stopping short of her orgasm, as her body trembles. It's the little things, like after a long stressful day she tell me to come here, (in the tone of voice that means it's ok, let me take care of you) after my shower, laying slightly on top of her, my shoulders draping her hip, my arms running up her sides with my hands behind her back, with my head just beneath her breasts as she rubs my head, and my neck, as we lay in silence.

Time with her seems effortless, she's my muse when I need inspiration, slave when I feel the urge to bring out the rope, freak when she wants Daddy's attention, and submissive when she gets his attention. And Daddy's cum canvas, at the end of it all. She's my Good Girl, and this is our story.

They met on a day that doesn't normally appears on the calendar, Words made it there for, and thought for sure she was going to be late, because when they talked previously she was further away then he was. After pacing for a while trying to collect his thoughts, she pulled in and quickly parked. As he starts walking towards her car she gets out to greet him. Taking a moment to take her in and her beautiful green eyes flared up at him. As he thinks she's a little smaller then what he's use to but let's see how this goes. She stood 5'7", even gentle shoulders, nice sized breast, nice hips that flows down to a nice ass, that I knew I'll enjoy spanking and a nice juicy pussy that bulged from the front of her nicely tight jeans. She had short blue and purple hair, when the sun hits it just right, with a gun clipped to her back, sexy saharan fire ball, just ready to kick some ass. Walking into the restaurant that was tucked away, perfect place for a first meet, friendly staff and quiet atmosphere perfect for getting to know someone.

Chapter 2
Sign Of The Unicorn
Double Edge

I want to reach out to you, I want to for once know that you know I mean the best, and that you're endlessly the one I want to share this all with.. But how can I when I don't trust you? How can I trust that you'll have my best intentions at heart? How can I trust that in the end you won't fuck me over, for everything you feel you're worth? In my head I've talked to you over and over, I've reached out to you and all for what? For you to deny me? For you to walk away? All for what? For your family to continue to use you? Out of fear that I won't do right for you and my son? What do I do? How can I shake this? Why can't/couldn't you see I've always had your heart, mind and soul better well being before my own?? Why must I fear something that should be easy, that should be logical.. Why must I live another day without you??

Sign of the Unicorn

Magical how its presence can stand for so much. Hope (for a better tomorrow)

Love (for which is rare, in fairytales love ends with a happily ever after, and in life it's only once in a life time you find that one person that brings your life clarity, brings your life true meaning).

Truth (for which all things are clear, honesty to yourself, and everyone around you. Truth is the one thing to completely set you free, free to hope, free to love, free to explore self-worth)

Self Worth (something we all lose sight of and sometimes it takes the unicorn to bring it out of you, for you to love yourself, to be able to look at yourself in the mirror and see who your meant to be, to see your self at your happiest, to see that smile, that glow, that sexy, perfection that have been neglected through the years, tears that have fallen, finally wiping them away and seeing the happiness that you deserve..)

Freedom (let yourself be free, free to hope, love, trust, be honest, know that you're worth more then anything on this planet, in this lifetime or the next. Let your freedom be worth having, worth living for!!)

Satisfaction (this is a huge one, for all the lifetimes we spend in search of a unicorn we get lost, we forget, we pretend that we know. But true satisfaction is when it's reawakened and it shines through, bursting from every pore, shining brighter than the sun. From the first touch, first kiss, you've never known ecstasy until something magical appears, the level of satisfaction, taking you to new heights, giving you highs you never knew existed, and with just three words and calm any storm, silence any soul, sooth the roughest tightest skin, and break down any walls that may stand in its way.)

I am The Unicorn, the bringer of hope, love, peace, and silence.

Sign

Forever & a Lifetime

Forever and a lifetime have I've waited to find you!!

Waiting to love you!!

Forever and a lifetime I've waited to hold you!!

Waited to make you mine, forever and a lifetime..

Forever and a lifetime I've waited patiently, hopelessly, forever dreaming of the day you return to me.

Return to this home here in my arms for a lifetime forever in this lifetime and the next

I've waited forever and a lifetime for you!!

Can't help but feel

I can't help but to feel your tears streaming down your face, lonely waiting to be wiped away.

I can't help but to feel your heart pounding, aching, feeling like it's about to jump out of your chest.

I can't help but to hear your thoughts, whispering to me in the darkness like the darkest secret fighting to escape.

I can't help but to feel your body, as it aches from the loneliness in the night air..

I can't help but to feel you, because we are one and our souls call to each other as unicorns call to their mate..

Nothing to Give

There's so many things I could say, but do I dare to say them? Do I dare to think them? But instead I'll whisper I love you in the dark under my breath carefully so my demons don't hear me.. If I can't be with you then I'll lock my heart away for all of eternity never bearing your name again, so there will be no missing of your sweet name rolling across my lips, no memories of my hands rolling across your hips, for they'll be locked until the day you return and set them free.. Eternity (to be continued)

Paradise

In her eyes he found paradise. No, not the false pretenses of paradise but the paradise that he has grown to know, love, and ultimately long for. The golden flecks that reminded him of a summer day by the beach that gently faded into this blue that reminded him of the sky he use to gaze at while floating in the ocean watching as the clouds lazily pass by. That deep blue that reached out to this really wonderful green that reminded him of the palm trees that whispered to him in the wind. Paradise. Paradise where only he knew he could find peace. Peace in the wind that swayed like her hips anytime he saw her walk. You know the sway you only imagine you would see in the wind if you could only see it blow. True paradise where he lived for so long but took for granted because of the bad times that followed. But briefly he was home again, in that moment in time where things were right again, looking in her eyes reminded him of paradise...

Oh how I wish

Oh how I wish I could take her worries away...

Ease her mind so her inner demons would just leave her alone...

Oh how I wish,

Wish that I could mend her soul and take away all that haunts her in her loneliest hours...

Oh how I wish

Wish I could take away all of her bad, sad, and depressing, memories that haunt her at night...

Oh how I wish...

Oh how I wish I could take her into my arms never to let go, fulfill her every desire as if it's my own...

Yes I wish!!

I wish this all for you, for you are my guiding light and there's not enough words in the world to truly express my feelings for you..

Where it Starts

It all started with a touch..

A first kiss..

A smile

And love..

In the beginning it was passion that brought me to you, pulling me closer to you like two magnets drawn to each other.

Closer and closer, until finally my hand stroked down your back, across your spine as you melted for the first, in what seems like a very long time. From that touch we both knew we were destined to be together...

Looking into your eyes, seeing that smile that turned my world upside down, I remember thinking how perfect!!

As you left me, I remember wishing you were near, hoping I would bump into you again. I remember that single touch, that smile, and from there I knew it was love..

A love unlike any other, a love that can with stand the strongest storms, death, and anything imaginable for as long as we're together in this lifetime or the next you're all I could ever need!!!

Unseen Lover

Bubbling, disruptions of the heart, aching, burning with love and hatred, wanting nothing more then to be in your embrace. To look in your eyes, to smell your sweet scent, to hear your laughter face to face. Drunken off of hate from not having you and hating the one I love for having your love. A love so beautiful but so violent disrupting the forces of nature, destroying everything in its path. When the path of love is open, the path of our inner most desires could be possible. Instead theres bubbling, disruptions of the heart, aching, burning with love and hatred, wanting nothing more then your embrace.

Moon

My moon is bright, it's clear and it lights my life in ever way possible. My moon brings me joy, cools me under the night sky, loves me in a way i didn't know it was possible..

Dear moon

For you I

I'm grateful, grateful for the joy you bring, the clarity you bring me in the night sky.

Oh moon how can I thank you for the freedom you provide and the guidance in your gentle embrace...

Dear moon

I haven't seen you for quite some time now, I'm lonely here in this bed, alone in the dark without your beams to keep me company, to keep me safe from this demon that comes into my room and touches me and hurts me with no one to tell. Oooh moon bring me light, rescue me from this life and take me into your warm embrace... P.s. I miss you

Dear Mo–o–n dammit...

Dammit moon how come you won't shine for me?! It's been a little over two weeks and all i see is darkness, and clouds!! Why must you leave me alone?! When things were perfect you were here! I was happy!! What must i do to bring you back to me?!! I can't take this life any longer moon!! Not that you care, I've took a bottle of sleeping pills I need an escape...

Dear Heather

I am here even when you cant see me, I'm here holding you. Heather.. Heather?!!! Nnooooo !!! Heather!! WHAT DID YOU DO HEATHER!!! NOOOOOOO

Lifetime of Love

With a kiss her worries went away, instantly her storm calmed and dissipated, he could see the changes within her. Watching the peace in her eyes grow while he wiped away her tears. To discover that she has been the one he has been waiting for, for so long, all the dreams in the dark slowly came to light. The pit of death in his soul slowly started filling with every tear he wiped away. "Lisa," he mumbled as she looked up with eyes bluer then any ocean, "Yes?" she replied as he pulled her closer, kissing her taking her breath away, in her breathless moment she realized this isn't that dream that keeps her up at night inches away from screaming. She realized in that moment that he's the one she couldn't live without. Years later, standing at his funeral with a smile on her face, and love in her heart she speaks softly to him "thank you for the best years a woman could ever ask for, three kids, and all the memories, the things we've learned, and I've learned from you i'll cherish forever. Standing there strong, with a heart of gold, i'll never forget you my love," remembering his warm embrace against her skin, with him whispering i'll never be without you. The rest of her life she lived with him alive in her, until her heart of gold gave out.. and even then she went with a smile on her mumbling I'm on my way my love, see you soon...

You Belong

You belong to me, your mind, heart, and soul...

You belong to me from head to toe, every curve from your full lips to the crease between your beautiful toes..

You belong to me

From the first time i made you smile, to the first sigh from the thoughts of loving me.

You.. Belong

You belong to me, for you're my Queen and i worship you.

These Arms

These arms are made to hold you,

Imagine you coming home to me, after a long day of work, slow music going, then you come around the corner to me making you dinner, with a hot bubble bath. Leading you to the bath, undressing you slowly, watching you as you step into the tub and have a seat. I come sit behind you and ask about your day while massaging your day away. I love how your body respond to my every touch, as i tell you i love you with every kiss, and caress, as we talk and i hold you close, feeling your nails rub across my skin, your hands as you grip my arms to lay closer to my heart for where it beats for you, the feeling of your skin next to mine, feeling you drive me insane, your love leaves me needing more, and awaiting your next touch.

Restless

Laying in one spot while my mind is a million and one places, legs twitching, body rocking, mind blowing, neck breaking speeds of thoughts through my head. I close my eyes there's flashes of you, your body against mine, smelling you all over me, it reminds me i need to shower, but it's 3am and all i want to do is go back to sleep. Debating should i get up to go shower now? Or wait until a little later? As you lay here curled up beside me, I'm tempted to wake you up to ask if you would like to join me in a shower. But i don't because i remembered that you haven't been sleeping well. A thousand questions rush through my mind, along those questions pops up well what should i do now? Shower? Bath? Scream? Well in my head I'm screaming from the mountain top i just want to sleep, fighting back the urge to cry, fighting back the urge to cut on the tv and xbox one to see who's online to take my frustration out on, fighting back the urge to wake you up and ask would you like to take a shower with me. Then my thought falls to two women who have both caught my interest on the left is one I've been talking to for a while that wants what she wants but won't give an answer to what i want, debating if i should end it or not before i lose interest. Then the one on the right (let's just call her the tease) goofy, attractive, that sneaks through my mind and steal my thoughts like a ninja meanwhile hearing her laugh as she does so. Man i really should get up and shower. Then out of the darkness i hear a whisper what you doing? Before i knew it, i answered with one word, dammit that was my chance to ask if she wanted to join me for a shower... Ugh restless, with nowhere to go, nothing to do, and no one to talk to... Lol restless...

Unique

Hello, some of you may know me as Demetri, or the magical unicorn that just appeared, or a magnificent dream that you don't want to be awakened from. But I'm just simply what ever you need when you need it. Im the one who makes you wonder when you can't figure me out, I'm the one who gives you what you want, but yet leaving you wanting for more. I'm the one that make you do things you wouldn't believe, I'm the one who makes you wonder how you ended up pantyless standing in front of me...

Im the depth of your ocean when you're stuck out at sea, I'm your pillow when you cry at night, I'm your renegade when you need a place to hide, and your rock when you need a place to climb...

Im simply me, whatever you need, i am now and forever will simply be.

Sign

Unique the Bull

ONE

One heart, one mind, one soul

In my hands is your heart, free to love, live, and grow.

Grow into me, into my heart so we can be as one.

One, together, one mind, one heart, one soul.

One soul gliding through life, under the wings of love.

Love with no end, that knows no bounds, that lives forever.

Pen

Give me a pen and I'll write away your worries.

Give me a pen so I can write you a new dream, where all you ever do is smile and be happy.

Give me a pen

Give me a pen so I can write out your life.

Give me a pen so I can make all your dreams come true

Give me a pen and I'll take you on a journey to places you've never been.

Give me a pen...

Give me a pen and I'll explore your body inch by inch, line by line, curve after curve, only so I can show you that you're perfect in so many words.

Give me a pen for my words isn't only black and white, because it's all the colors of the rainbow and it lives inside of you.

Give me a pen!!

Think of you

I think of you...

I think of you when you're sleeping in the next room.

I think of you even when I'm sleeping and you're in my dreams.

I think of you...

I think of you when I can't sleep.

I think of you even when I get weak.

I think of you...

I think of you when you're away.

I think of you even when memories in my head play.

I think of you because in my heart you'll forever stay.

When I think of you, it brightens my day!!!

Heart Pressed

How do i say i love you without sounding to heart pressed, how do i say i miss you without my eyes tearing up? How can i hug you without sinking into you and losing myself. How do i? How do i love you so deep that my soul cracks a little deeper with the simplest thought of you. How can i cry in front of you without my tears staining your skin with my love. How can i love you so deep that i blindly walk through life not knowing which direction I'm going...

I Miss

I miss the moments we use to have, i miss the shine of your smile as i hear you laugh, i miss all the times i removed your hair from your face, softly caressing your skin in the process. I miss the sound of your voice in my ear like a sweet melody from my favorite song. I miss how my name rolled across your tongue and fumbled out of your mouth lol (oh how i miss that) i miss my friend, my love, my peace of mind you provided.

Remember when

Sitting here thinking back, back to that one track, the track that plays loudly but soothing in the back, back of the track grinding, grinding to the falsetto of your voice, holding you close as it get wetter, wetter as the rain fall with the stroke of lightning, highlighting your Silhouette, thinking back to your shadow when we first met, having you right now in this moment kinda feel like a lucky bet, a lucky bet that have been set, as The tempter rise wile clinching your thighs so turned on you feel me getting harder and harder between your thighs, as the tempter rise sweat droplets starts to run off your chest moaning with every caress, chest to chest feeling your breast as you come to a rest, in my arms, safe away from any harm, you'll never get cold, you in my arms will keep you warm

Sea Love

As deep as the depths of the ocean..
Meaning my love knows no boundaries, there's no end that you can see, and very few have made it to that point. My love is beautiful, its gentle, will consume you, and will amaze you with how vast it may be. My love knows no beginning nor ending, it just is.. Love (4 letters simple meaning, strong feeling) as deep as the depths of the ocean (27 letters, a meaning you can only imagine, a feeling as strong as a wave that destroys everything in it's path.) my love is strong, it doesn't waver, it's forever lasting.. AS DEEP AS DEEP OF THE DEPTHS OF THE OCEAN

Weakness

From the touch of your skin to the taste of your lips, sweetness like a dream, floating from cloud to cloud, forever lasting, floating like a castaway on the sea of your love.

Love so deep the deepest ocean can't compete, forever in your love, deep, as deep as can be In you. My love knows no boundaries, no limit to what i can do in my love for you.

You are my breath of fresh air, my light at the end on a tunnel, the water that keeps my ship afloat, the breeze against my tingling skin. You... You are the thought from the time the Sun comes up, to the time the Sun goes down.. You are my direction when i have none, my balance when i can't stand. You... Are... My... Warmth that burns within that keep me going so i can be a better me tomorrow then i was today....

Missing You

Saying I miss you is an understatement, as each passing day I long for you, my heart beats to my lonely tears for you, to what appears to be never ending until I have you in my arms. Words can't explain how often you run through my brain, I mean it's insane knowing how much you mean to me, not knowing when I hear from you again, or if you're still my friend, when will my worrying end? Is it where my love end and start to die from not being your friend, slowly counting the seconds until I take my last breath on the day, my life ends. And even then, I will still long to be your friend, never breaking my promise to love you until the end. In you I found out where I began, a new lover and friend, how to love to the very end, and how to become a better man. Missing you is the truth and where I stand now, close your eyes I'll meet you in dream land...

Only for one night

If only for one night you were mine.

If only for one night we could stop time.

If only for one night I could hold you tight.

If only for one night I could make love to you and cater to you right.

If only for one night.

If only for one night I didn't wake up alone.

If only for one night I didn't have to stare at your picture in my phone.

If only for one night I could make everything right.

If I only had one night I would use it to hold you tight.

That Woman IS You

There's this woman that I love, she is the one I dream about day in and day out. She's the one that my heart beats a lonely solo for in love There's a woman that makes all my dreams come true, my breath of fresh air, the beginning to my end.

There's a woman that I love, that takes me through changes as my love for her grows, that makes my heart skip beat, for its lonely solo, my breath of fresh air, my beginning to the end, that makes all my dreams come true, that woman.. That woman is you!!

Romance

Let me look in your eyes & share your happiness. Let me feel your heart as it beat beneath my finger tips and filling you with love. Let me love you like there's no tomorrow, caress you as if time was ending and complete you as if your life depended on it. Let me kiss you missed you for a thousand years. Let me make your body tremble as if your climax was forever lasting. Let me touch your soul as you drift to heaven. Let me be your man and I'll show you real love and how to be touched with no hands.

Bonding & Belonging

Love is a complicated thing, it's a bond between two people that grows tighter with every action, that eventually led to the desire to belong to that special person that you've bonded with, in turn your hearts long for each other, begging to be closer, to feel the tension and desire for one another, and finally belonging to the other. All the heart want and pulls for is to be when it feels it belongs. The desire to feel wanted, to feel love is stronger as time passes on its ever lasting cycle of infinite standings. Love is a roller coaster, because it have its ups and downs, loops that everyone goes through but like a roller coaster all you have to do is hold on tight and last for the ride for it will always get better in the end. All we need to do is hold on.

Wish

I wish you could see your self through my eyes, I wish you could feel what I feel every time you're in my arms.I wish you could hear my thoughts if only for a moment when I see your face, as you light up with the simplest thought or sight of me, I wish I wish I could feel you as you're feeling me as you run your hands over my skin, if only I could hear your thoughts for a moment and see what you see when you look at me I wish... I wish if only for a moment...

A moment I could wish for.... If only there were one wish..

Love Betrayal

Never will I hurt you the way you've hurt me, not trusting that I'll put you first above anyone or thing feels dirty like a tar stain of betrayal. I would never force you into anything false due to my own pleasure selfishly I love you more than pleasure could ever amount to. Loving you more then I love my self, burns so deeply to my core I'm erupting with anger at your love betrayal. Oddly it seems like you don't know where your ex ends and where I begin. To love you means that I have to let go completely, to love you unconditionally means I would have to lose myself in you and close my eyes to all others. To support you meant to put all of my wants aside to ensure your happiness. But yet you mistake my love? Love betrayal

YOU

You are... You're my weakness, that causes my knees buckle with the slightest whisper of your name. You... you are my flame that burns brought within, that ignites my fuel to become a better man... you... you are, my sunshine that shines brightly through my dark and lonely clouds, reminding me there's always hope... you're... You're my hope for a better hour for a better tomorrow.. you.... You're everything that I could ever hope for in a woman, a lover, a wife and a friend... you.... are... You're my heart.... with you my heart dance, skips a beat, race with every kiss, and calms down with just your smile...

Flame

Every time you bite your lip, I look you in your eyes and see that beautiful smile from with in, you dig deeper and deeper into my heart. Every kiss, every tease, with every touch my soul catches fire.. With every laugh, my heart skips a beat and catches fire, with the sound of your voice my passion for you burns deeper, the deeper my passion burns the more you invade my body the more of you I have in me, the more I grow to love you as each day passes.. Thank you for being who you are, thank you for letting me in, thank you for helping me heal and grow..

Its Morning

Its morning, breakfast in bed careful not to disturb you as you rest you head, proudly cooking with all love that I was fed, the caressing and kissing making up for the time we been missing, wishing you were near, but now that you're here in my arms you'll always be near. My wife I welcome you home, we'll never have to spend life alone. After breakfast is over now you're wide awake come to the bathroom your shower await. Kissing you slowly and your cloths I take, enjoy your shower for your massages awaits. warm oils, and your soft skin, where do I begin? At your feet and then up I climb, up your legs as you unwind. Pass your thighs, to your hips, your lower back I kiss fulfilling your every wish, massaging your back up to your shoulders, releasing your stress, I'll love you always because you're the best..

Nice guys FINISH LAST

I saw on one of my friends status' that nice guys finish last because they put their woman first., First above any and everything is my woman, her every thought, feeling, emotion, and every small thing that matter to her, that the last nigga looked over. Nice guys finish last because they're woman is first in bed making love to her mind, then her heart, and soul, taking his time caressing her body while respecting every curve. Yea nice guys finish last, but we know how to achieve the biggest orgasms out of our women. Nice guys finish last because they put their woman first!

Chapter 3

Inspiration

Frustration v.s. Direction

In my frustration I write, I write to yell out against my unorganized, unorthodox, thoughts that keep me confined. Confined in this box where it rains random letters and numbers from this blue cloud that blocks out my sunlight, that forces me to lose my direction. Direction to the promise land where all is good and one's mental state can be free. Free to follow any direction at any time it pleases, without confinement. But yet my direction is blocked by this cloud that's slowly drowning me with unsynchronized letters, numbers, images that brings on more frustration. Frustration that drives me to go hunting for something thats not there, but yet i hunt anyway to keep me out of this box, with that rain cloud, that keeps haunting, blocking out my sunlight, blocking my direction, that leaves me screaming because I'm lost, while trapped in this box where random letters and numbers strikes, forming images of codes that i can't crack, losing my mind griping my hair as my mental cracks from the frustration of the loss of direction leaving me breathless, weightless and alone..

Give and Take

If there's one thing that life has taught me is that all things in life require give and take, nothing comes for free, there's always a price to be paid.. Yes things are given freely but eventually there will be a pay out. Might not be today or tomorrow but eventually.. Intentions are in the right place, and you may not know that you will need that person, but life is a circle what goes around will eventually come back to you.. Life is tricky that way from one life time to another it leaves you bread crumbs to catch up on..

So be careful in what you do or who you do it to for you circle will turn, sometimes it's in an instant, others may take you years.. Remember your circle, remember that everything in life comes with consequences, your actions causes reactions, your reactions can predict your future... Remember...

Painting

When you look at a picture of a scenic mountain it looks perfect huh?? But what you don't see are the dead trees and brush that are supporting the perfection you think you see. With out that you really wouldn't have the colors and contrasts you see and love. It's the mistakes and so-called dead stuff underneath that give it the life we see above Without death there isn't life, without life there isn't mistakes, if there aren't mistakes nothing else would be possible but death.

Island

At first i couldn't see it, from the trees, from the mountain, and everything i felt blocked my view. Until I closed my eyes and everything came into view. Clear, precise, beautiful as ever, nature calling loudly to be free. Alone there, on that island welcoming the breeze that flowed against me. Though my eyes are closed, I could see everything that the island had to offer me.

Standing there feeling the sun against my unforgiving skin , warmth within like I've never felt before. Feeling so alive and looking forward to the journey ahead of me. Scared but excited, alone but with out feeling it.

Touch

Within my touch you will find enlightenment, peace, and pleasure. Touch for me is more than just a physical and psychological connection, but a connection into your thoughts, and soul. Your future, your past, it's a bridge into your hopes and dreams, who you are to who you could be. Within my touch you will find healing, love, compassion, and the way to the path to forget your past. I welcome your touch, for your touch is the path to a new beginning.

Bloom place

Bloom- my place to grow, nurture, capitalized love held within, to grow, and be free.

Place- my place of origin, place to thrive and achieve mental freedom, my place of calmness, happiness, my place of mental stability.

Bloom place is the place of mental security/serenity, where all things love and thrive. With every beat of the heart, and every breath. Bloom place is where I live day in and day out, it's real, with no judgements, and where passion lives in perfect harmony with love.

Truth

Revealing secrets takes a strong heart, an understanding of what's soon to come, and must know that their admissions would test their relationship with friends, family and whoever else may be concerned. Now do you need to answer to these people? No!
Will it be scary to think what others may think? Yes, but you can't let that stop you, can't let fear control you!
Will it hurt to see others reactions? Maybe... The point of this is to ease your mind, it's to make you stronger and comfortable within yourself, to put your foot down and say enough is enough, this is who I am live with it or leave my life. This test will show you who's truly your friend, who loves you no matter what, and who is only in your life for a season. This will also test you, to see if you can live with yourself alone and truly be happy. This could also show you that those who in your life that loves you unconditionally that everything is going to be alright. We will all

work through this with you, then you know you have a solid team behind you. Don't let fear rule your life, set yourself free, live and be happy.

History: My Relationship to my wife

Growing up we are taught that there's the one person for you. We are taught all relationships are to be one on one. But growing up, expending my knowledge, setting my mind free, achieving ultimate freedom in one's space, you grow to realize it's not completely true. As we grow, we change, for the better or worse. Things complexly move around in life. But with this you come to realize that not one person is perfect. Not one person possesses all the qualities, beliefs, and interest as you, for some they just settle, but end up cheating because they are in search of what's missing, but there's others that can just settle and be happy, but then again as time goes on they become miserable because we're taught relationship is between two people. But there's that one percent of couples that are completely happy and will remain completely happy in their relationship. For those like me, completely complexed, that have accepted life for what it is, that changes every day that shoot higher than the moon that always making changes in life, growing, and seeing past what life have to offer. It requires someone who see things the same as I do, and I have that in my mate but like me there's a female essence missing from both of our lives. Sitting down talking about it, understanding that if this relationship is to work there can't be any secrets So we are one, her going against what she was taught, making decisions on her own without being judged, or anything set her free. With past relationships she always felt like something was missing but she didn't know what until she got with me, she learned she can be her self, explore who she is, and truly be free. With time she learned who she are, what she wanted, and what's missing and how to go about getting what she want She understand the feeling, there's one person in her past who if she had a chance to work things out with I wouldn't try to stop her I would support her, and the relationship However she is interested in finding a female mate, something she never had just that one friend, lover, sister that could fill the part of her that's missing Now to answer your question, why you? With you I learned that I can be myself, and that love goes so much deeper than the heart, you were my calm in my storm the one thing that was completely right and everything was wrong as long as I was with you nothing else mattered.

So Called system

I'm tired of spending money filing papers to this imperfect system, that allows the mother's to hide behind it, while denying a man the rights to seeing his child/children. Yesterday I spent the day looking through the self help portion of the clerk of the court family law division and the logic these people use to justify the actions that's being taken isn't right. What isn't right? You're probably wondering. So if a mother wanted to sign over their rights to their children only thing they have to do is write a letter stating that they world like to give custody to their mom (the kids grandparent) and have a notoriety stamp and sign it and send it into the courts and they're in the clear. I've seen it happen. Now the part that isn't right is if a man wanted to sign over his rights to a child that they'll never see again but pays child support for the court will deny him the rights to relinquish his rights to his child! They say it's for the well being of the child.

As the mother's get to gloat to they're family and friends "oh that nigga no good, I had to put him on child support" to make your self look good in front of your friends or feel good about your self.. Tired of the bias system where the woman is always right unless proving otherwise, now a woman can have their kids token away from them tho the dad may be stable it's still isn't granted that the dad would get custody The odds are 70 to 1. The courts would look to the grandparents before the dad. (Florida law!! see I knew the system were screwed up but not this bad.) The imperfect system that does nothing to help the fathers that actually want to be there for there for they're kids. But they guarantee that they pay child support. A man in this same system have to fight tooth and nail in order just to get visitation rights. Now for the guys that have kids but doesn't want to have anything to do with their kids or don't care one way or another rather they see their kids or not get the red carpet, get to go y in with their life's with little to no repercussions. Imperfect system, no bias system!! This popular system that vows it's the best thing for the kids and the mother, but no one sees the downside, no one knows the downsize, no one knows that hurt that goes behind this system that doesn't give a fuck about those involved, it's a one sided story, just another paper across another desk.. I have two boys Jeremiah and Tyrese I've spent countless years in Florida trying to be closer to them. Tyrese I didn't find out about him until a year after he was born. I found out through the child support system lol his mom wasn't putting me on child sorry but his grandmother was. After it was confirmed I picked up my life to move closer (moved back to Polk county) I went to visit, and were never greeted warmly, there were always the threat of the cops being called, so I've filed for joint custody about 6 different times believe it or not the last hearing almost landed me in jail, and the judge starting a man/boy (giving my age at the time) don't know anything about raising a child. So months later I petition for visitation supervised/unsupervised about 4 times 14 or 15 years later still no visitation, but still on child support.. Jeremiah mom and I were good friends I've done every thing I could think of to make things work. I've offered to be there I was there when he was born, but when it was time to deliver she picked her mom to be there by her side ("she deserved it" so I was told) I stick around visited but only on his mom terms, I had to have sex of some form to continue to see him. I wanted more then the sex. For some of you that would work, if I had been foolish it would've worked but it's not right. Years past after I left Florida to better my self and mend my heart I offered to move them where I was, I offered to get her her own place, even told her she could bring the guy she was with at the moment. Recently my now wife and I offered to move her here, we were financially ready to put our selfs in a hole just for once to have him closer we offered to get her a place for them, we were willing to get a second car so they could get around. Her response was shocking in the lease (I got cursed out lol then she stopped talking to me.) Time past I got marred then got slapped with a child support order. I've said all this to bring up my point for before. I've done everything I could to make things work, even played by the rules of the system, it does nothing to help fathers who cares, the fathers that want to make a difference.. This is the only way I know how to fight back against this system people love. This is my life my truth, this is my situation..

Expectations

The thing about expectations is no-one will ever add up to what you want of them, what you think they should be, not one human is perfect that's what make us who we are. (Unique) The moment you expect something of someone you set that person up to fail. Expectations closes your heart, makes you blind, and opens room for judgement. Rather you realized it or not you can really hurt the one/ones you Love with expectations. Key to life is to love/accept the one's you Love because they love you more and need you more than you think.

Fools Gold

I'm on this road slowly coming to a stop, formulating a plot not to stop on this dead-end course, constructing a morse code for this road, to unfold the many stories untold. I refuse to fold to the road with stories untold that I must unfold out in the cold. Sold by my collective thoughts and route after route thought after thought I saw the truth, deep down in my roots I found the boot that kicked my ass and sent me on this journey, slowly learning while burning within that's how I ended up here in this dead end trying to make amends, for my past sins, it's my untold story being told now that I'm seventy-six years old.. Speak up and speak loud let the sound of your voice get carried by the clouds. Speak out and let your story be told, you don't want to be like me out in the cold as your story unfold, be bold and don't be sold on a story like fool's gold. For you have the controls

Inspiration

Inspiration: have many faces that shows up when you're not looking for it

Crazy, time to rhyme what's in my mind, time to show the divine power of the hour watching my words build higher the a tower, blooming like a flower beneath the tombs that boomed the room that soon conceived me, to see what all I have grown up to be, from he who have made the world and all his people are free, free to be all that they see, only question is, what to be? You see me the one he delivered unto you to remind you to have faith and you'll get through, for he is your spiritual glue. For the end of your life you'll get what's due not because of me but because you've done what he's asked of you.

Writing

Writing to me is natural it's like breathing.. It grants me instant gratification as I write chemicals release producing dopamine the feeling of wow or love as a well written piece comes together as the endorphins surge through my veins my sciences happen narrowing down my sight shaping my focus as my thoughts flows from my mind like a water fall, matching concepts to music, music to beats, leveling the playing field so that people can relate.. As I put together phrases that grasp your attention as if you were sitting right in-front of me listening to me words flow from my lips.. I don't just write for attention I write because it's a part of me knowing that I can provide a service to people is all the gratification that I need.. In my writing I pull the people into my world, my mind to help the escape, decompress, release build up tension, and gives then someone to cuddle up to with in their mental space.. Some day my book will be on everyone night stand, book shelf, it will be the one thing people will talk about and share with their friends it will be the little shine of hope to the right person in the night when they need, it will be their friends when they need it.. Not because I say so.. But because I relate to people as they relate to me, my words come with conviction, pain, love, and inspiration, I've struggled, I've been broken, I've been where allot of people are going to go and have been, I don't write because I claim to be great, I write because I can relate on a broad spectrum of topics...

Late Night Gospel

Up again, can't sleep, it's quiet in here not a peep. Time for my mind to take a leap, through history to refresh what time have to teach. Pulling my hopes and dreams back within reach. I remember a message that a preacher preached, ending with "never let your dreams get to far that you cannot reach!" See it took me awhile to understand that message that he preached, didn't know that God had me within his reach.. See I was big headed and chuckled smiling thinking "there's not a dream that I can't reach" not here I am later thinking back and reflecting, never think you're in charge of your life while neglecting the man who gave you life, point you to the left when you want to go right. Growing up I ran from his anointing, putting up a fight but yet he creep in and speaks through me when I write. Let's get back to those dreams I was talking about, the things I have on my check list it was quite an amount. But now it's only two or three.. Out of all things I've wanted to be, he would only allow me to just be me.. Everything I wanted to do, I just want it, but not to impress you. To the day my dreams is complete I know that God will walk with me..

Me...... I...... Us

Polyamory- A person with more then one mate, or life partner. I tend to wonder about this, more now then ever.. Why you ask? Typically satisfaction comes with one partner/mate in a perfect world. Sure love is typically between two people, but if you have enough love, and love strong enough it's possible to love two people unconditionally, fully as if it were just you and one other, these relationships are just as successful as any other relationship/marriage. Morally, you may think it's wrong, you may even judge the ones who practice polyamory, fact of the matter is this isn't a perfect world, it's no different then gay marriage, lesbian relation-ships, or bi curious female/male. You can't count it as cheating because they will know about each other, more then likely live under the same roof, and would most likely have their girls night/spa day out together. At this point in my life I have one person in my life that's not going any where, wether anyone likes it or not, I feel I'm to a point that I'm ready to share my life with who I want and do as I want as long as I'm not hurting anyone in the process be happy. Alright, good night everyone that's all I have to say on this subject..

Dream come true

My dreams came true the moment I met you. Your grace, your smile, that sexy ass style. While all the while I couldn't break my smile, as our eyes locked, time froze, no tick no tock. Smell so sweet, beautifully filling the street. I knew it was my time, time to react. If I fuck up now, time would never go back, so I took a min to think clearly before I react, wisely planning how can I attack, speak calmly, but not too smooth, don't want her to think that I'm a Mack. Speaking softly drawing her in, as I extended my hand, speaking my name clearly making sure she hears, complement her beauty, and the earrings in her ears. She smiled softly, and with a warm tone thank you she said, as her voice whispered softly through my head. This is one I cannot let go as I whispered in my head. Time went on with none to spare asking her to Marry me on one knee with a diamond ring that held a glare!!! As she scream yes jumping up and down, my queen as I landed her with her crown... Let this be a lesson for those who wait, BELIEVE, & TRUST IN GOD, AND HE'LL PREDICT YOUR FATE!!!!!

Sex on the beach

Mmmmm sex the beach, so smooth, soothing, strong and one of the best things. Sweet tasting like an exotic peace of fruit, perfect height, nice round ass, beautiful and rare like a wild flower that only blooms in the most remote island. I'll take it on the rocks, perfect body, holding the flavors together like a fine wine ready to be tasted. Like a brand new car sexy ready to be taken for a spin. Damn i love my sex on the beach can i get another round on the bar???!!

Peaceful Therapy

Hello welcome to peaceful therapy, my name is Demetri and I'll be your therapist for today. We're going to start with you taking your shoes off, allow yourself to get comfortable as your feet sink into my plush carpet. Make yourself at home feel free to get as comfortable as you can. This session is all about you, your needs, desires, and releasing of all of your stressors. We can take all the time you need, take it slow and allow it to unwind.

Today session we will begin in the kitchen. Now if you would allow me to pick you up and sit you on the counter, like so. We are ready to get started.

Where would you like to start?

What do you feel you need right now?

What's your desire?

What stresses you?

As she sits there thinking I'm drying my hands. Reaching over grabbing the wok from its rack mounted to the wall. "What are you doing?" she asked "cooking" I replied ever so lightly with a comforting smile on my face. "What are you making?" "A little comfort food." (Hoping that the smell would trigger some memories.) Do you like red, green or yellow bell peppers in your food? I asked politely "red is fine" she replied taking a deep breath afterwards. As I began to dice the bell we started. Started with the love of the smell of the red bell peppers. Reminded her of her grandmother who died earlier this year at the age of 93. Story after story, tears flowed down her face, until she reached a point and smiled watching the weight lift from her shoulders. "Oh, the memories" she said with a tear rolling down her face wiping the tear away with a Kleenex. "Oh my god" she said with a very concerning look on her face. With out saying a word I looked at her and lightly said "continue" careful not to alarm her. "I never shared those memories with anyone" she mumbled. With a slight smile reassuring her that it's okay, asking her to take a deep breath and let it go. As the aroma fills the room taking in a deep breath she feel inclined to continue talking as time goes on. The completion of the food drawing near, you can start to see the changes on her face as she smiles more, posture straighten, head is a lot higher, vocal tone has risen, and she doesn't see life as bad as she used to. This experience has given her a new sense of hopefulness, to continue life, I encourage her to experience life, to go out and have fun. As the plates come out for service, her family walks into the dining area, she looks at me frightened, I reply "It's all going to be just fine you will get through this." As everyone sits down for the meal her mother asks "What kind of therapist are you?!" Looking over her glasses. "I'm an individual/family therapist committed to help-ing individuals and families through difficult times." I reply with a smile. My client passes around notes she has written to her family last Thursday (a week ago) during her last visit. As the notes are passed around the table, I explain to each family member why they were there and goals we were planning to meet each week. A family is a foundation build on love, trust, compassion and blood. Family is the glue to an individual existence in the world that makes society a better place. Upon reading each note, each individual had to give some type of feedback plus a goal that they would like to meet for each week. As the meal was done each family member spoke and cleared the room one by one until it was only one left. My client's mom Linda. "I just want to thank you for everything you have done so far," she explained. "It's been so hard losing my mother, everyone took it so bad, I... I, guess we all just grew apart. Calmly replying it's okay we all know what's it like to have lost a loved one. Reassuring her with a hug she thanked me again and walked out of the room. Moral of this story is: Life is precious, value it, let go of the things that hold you down, keep your head up, stand strong, and live life to the fullest.

Remember Me

Remember me not for the things that I did wrong,
Remember me not for the heart aches from my death, because I lived a full faithful life,
Remember me for my smile, the simple lessons that I tough
Remember me
Remember me for my actions the differences that I made.
Remember me for the thoughts, feelings that I left behind impacting everyone that I've met over my course of time.
Remember me
Remember me for the love that I've shared.
Remember me
Remember me for the words spoken, my actions, my lessons, my thoughts, my love and my directions that I've headed to get to where I am now, do dry your eyes, for I will always be with you in your heart, your thoughts, and with you every step you take.. Remember me

Half Way

You wonder where I am, but I'm at the halfway mark waiting for you to meet me there. You say I'm never there when you need me, but I assure you my child I'm here through every step, you curse me when you're having problems, but I'm here my child I'm the reason you don't crumble when the weight of the world is on your shoulders. You ask, "but why Lord?" I reply, "I've told you I'm here, meet me at the halfway mark walk with me, let me lead you, guide you in the right direction." I can't make this life easy for you, you have to meet me halfway, do for yourself, fight the battle uphill meet me halfway and I assure you I'll be at your back as you fight your way to me!! "Try my child, push my child I love you trust in me not man I will show you the way. Put one foot in front of the other and March to my name, praise my name, tell people about me, follow me but first you have to meet me halfway..."

God's Work

Sometime life throws you curve balls, sometimes it throws blizzards in front of you, for you to go through. Through thick and thin you must remain strong. The more you feel like damned if you do damned if you don't, is when you have to fight the hardest. Life may put up some resistance but that's when you must push harder, and harder until it moves in your favor. Having faith when it seems like there's no tomorrow makes you stronger, when it's dark out and stormy remember joy comes in the morning light, be patient, keep the faith, with every obstacle comes a lesson, with that lesson comes wisdom. You must go through some things to be born a new version of yourself. Remember go through and come out new. Everyone has a storm, it's all in the matter of how you handle the storm. Are you prepared??

Drunken Love

One night I was leaving the bar, walking home because I didn't live that far. Block after block my body leaned and rocked. Staggering still getting closer to home, I see someone sitting all alone, pausing for a moment to stay on my feet, as she stood up instantly my heart skipped a beat. Slowly swaying to stay on my feet I was determined to reach her with out feeling defeat. Excuse me miss what's your name? With out a pause she relied Christian. Feeling foolish I quickly explained you're simply beautiful, I just had to know your name. She laughed with a voice as soft as a feather, I asked would you like to go some where to get out of this weather? With a smile she suggest to go our separate ways, find me again once you sober up, then she wrote her name and number on my cup. Thinking to my self I have the best luck.. Two days later as sober as i could be, I noticed she moved in the building across the street from me. With out hesitation I searched for my cup, I couldn't find it with no such luck.. A week has passed now, missing her with every breath, my heart dropped with the news of her tragic death, back to the bar to drink my sorrows away but I couldn't get my drink down because I heard her voice say. Do not be sad and drink your life away, I love you John and I'll never go away, no drinks for me every since that day I've been sober for ten years now, living life and getting stronger with every living day.

Words

Sooo. I was talking to a co-writer, and the topic of how important words are and how a story from a different person perspective can be impactive, and just what someone else may need to hear. Words, experiences, life, are meant to be shared, because you never know who life you may leave an impression on. This is why I write, why I have a separate account just for my writing. I love getting the random messages of how something I wrote spoke to someone or how relatable it was.

Chapter 4

Relax

Ocean

I Love the sound of the waves clashing against the shore, as the waters rush up the sand, brushing against your skin washing all the worries away, taking you deeper into a trance. The moon slightly lit is setting the mood. Wind brushes you ever so slightly almost caressing your skin, in the stars you can see your life play like a sweet romance movie.. With the water, it makes all the things in life better.. Ocean take me away...

Story In The Wind

Blowing, cooling, whispers pass my ears, singing quietly, gently passing my head, caressing it with every passing moment. Gentle into the night, feeling you brush over me as I lay here. Give me chills all over. Hearing laughter off into the distance, brings tears to my eyes. Happiness moments I've shared with you. From the moment you were born you brought me joy, the mini tears I've wiped from your eyes, until you drove away to college, taking my heart and soul with you. I can still hear your voice echoing through the house, your laughter as it grew and matured with you, the broken heart we talked through over ice cream, and all the goodnight kisses we shared. Now in my old age, fulfilled life, and complete journey. Laying here under this night sky I say good night. Wind take me home, blow by ashes over the land, and may my voice forever be with her, as will be many lessons, the laughter, and my soul. For I have done my best to make her into the woman she is...

Life Poetry

Life poetry is a part of everyone in every day..it flows like the deepest emotion vibing to the sweetest beat. Making love to life like Marvin Gaye, let's get it on... Poetry flow through my veins as smooth as my blood, riding to the beat as sweet as usher's there goes my baby. Mystical flows giving me butterflies like floetry.. With skies as blue as the ocean, wind blowing through my soul, as if blowing a jazz horn, to a smooth rhythm as fingers snap to the beat... Life poetry as pure as my love in its rarest form. As I speak, flowing my lyrics twisting and flip my tongue like busta rymes on the hottest beat, my love for poetry, is like my love for music, and my people this is my life poetry.

Baby Girl

It all started with love, happiness, and a desire. Month after month we witched you develop, and grow, as time ticked on time neared for you to come out and meet the world, and the first site of your new parents.. Time ticked on til the day you arrived.. So small, beautiful, precious in every way. Looking you in your face in a unbelievable state, as you cry ensuring the room that you're ok. My baby girl, as your mom take you into her arms with so much joy, glowing with so much warmness... Meeting you for the first time is a moment that will be cherished for ever, for you are my baby girl and daddy love you for ever......

Night Air

Mmmmm, so calm, nice slight breeze. The tingling from the moistness in the night, relaxing and somehow massaging the worries from my day away, clearing my mind with every fresh breath... Aaahhhh... Quietly... listening to the wind as it wisp past me caressing against my skin gently... as I close my eyes slightly with a smile on my face, my very own home away from home... Aaahhhh... Night air...

Two in One, Perfect Wave

It's early morning. Sitting on my bored waiting for the sun to start to rise as the wind blows through my hair as the waves build, as the memory of the power runs through my mind reminding me of rocket, so smooth fast the rush of having so much power under me.. Sitting here waiting for the perfect moment the wave that I can just see my name on the one just for me, hearing the wave and the air around me as I find my way to the funnel as the wind blows my hair as I zig and zag tempting fait, feeling the water slide through my finger tips, feeling so free, nothing matter, nothing else exist, it's just me and my wave, this moment... As I call out to the wave like a much needed orgasm, as my satisfaction builds, like being on a track toping out my car easing in and out of curves drifting, as an orgasmic yyyyeeeeeessssss runs through my head reaching 3G in my turn as the hair on the back of my neck starts to rice but just as sudden as it start it's over.... The best ride ever..

That Feeling

I know that feeling of being alone, being in your head screaming hoping someone will finally hear you and come help you out of it.

I know the feeling of loneliness and in order to quiet that demon is to constantly surround yourself with people so you can no longer hear them whisper to you.

I know the feeling of desire, burning within so hot that it makes your flesh crawl and you start to feel goose bumps on the surface of your skin, I know. Because I have them too..

I know the feeling of crying to yourself for minutes on end, not for a particular other then you're just lost in your feelings and all you can do is cry. It's ok I know..

I know the feeling of crying for the one you love, missing em to the verge of tears, wishing/hoping that they'll... Just... Show up... On your door step... Repeating please just show up...

I know... I know the feeling of restlessness, can't see because he or she is on your mind and every time you close your eyes their right there next to you, so you quickly open them back to a lonely room with no embrace to warm you.. Yea I miss that too..

But it's ok, because I know. I know what you're going through because I feel them too..

I know those feeling, because I feel the same about you!!!

Chapter 5

NUMB

Reckless

Waiting around like a ticking time bomb, toxic to myself, death to others. Exploding without a purpose, reckless like a car speeding at fifty-five miles per hour with no driver. I am death like a poisonous gas building up in an empty house awaiting my next victim. I am havoc, drifting through life swirling to hit everything and one as if I was collecting money in the game of point. I am destruction, blowing things up at a notice turn. Turn your head for a second and you'll turn back to nothing but flames, and the smell of gasoline lingering through the air. I'm the night crawler, hunting you in your sleep, wrecking your dreams, killing all that's right within you... Because I AM!!!

Over

Your happiness means the world to me and I wish you nothing but the best.. as of myself, my feeling isn't up for topic, debate, or available information... just me, just my personality, nothing personal against anyone this is how I stay sane.. like all things in life it must come to a end, end, end of a cheaper in this book of life, end, end of the season for which my life needed improvement, end of the lessons to be learned.. with the awaking of myself, remembering who I am and where I came from.. now to reform my paradox, create a new limbo to dwell, reframe from this peaceful path that I've been on.. lets be honest I'm destructive I love my havoc, my pain, and taking the trash of those that serve no purpose.. I am havoc, that dwells in a paradox somewhere between this world and limbo

24

All I need is 24 hours, sit by the beach and cry under the stars and let my sorrows flow away into the sea, all I need is to release all my stress, pollution I let gunk my once clean world. All I need. All I need is 24 hours to be free to be me, with no limitations, distractions, no voices in my head, or the back of my neck, reminding me of all that I'm trying to get away from. All I need. All I need is, is 24 hours to pull myself together, escape, peace of mind, to cry for freedom, to be me and clean my once perfect world, with no limitations... 24 hour is needed.

Tonight

Tonight is the night for drinks, starting with my old friends Jack and Jim, as we stare and a mutual friend Hennessy with her fine ass thinking we should get together and have a three sum. Oh the mixes we would make!! Followed by that award friend Mr. Grey with his goose following that 57 Cabernet, looking at each other and thinking this is going to be a wild party. Maybe just maybe we should go tribal and call over Kailua to set things off properly.. Ah what the hell bartender!! Waste my drink, perhaps i can Smirnoff of my pants, while making my way to the bathroom stall with Chardonnay following behind, waiting to go into my mouth and scream through my system.. One hell of a party i think to my self ..

Senses

For a moment let's take away our senses, let's take the way that you feel, let's take away your thoughts and just breathe, close your eyes, and forget everything that you know, relax and just let go... trust me and let me lead you to a place of no regrets, where boundaries don't exist...

Tears of the willow

Tears of the willow

Sweeping in the wind

Slightly whispering in the wind

Under the wings of the bird flying by the willow

Sweeping through the wind

Swiftly through the leaves of the willow

Flows the tears of the willow

In the tears of the willow is love

Love for all who have been blessed with its presents

In it's tears there's hope

Hope of love, hope of a better tomorrow

Hope of all the fears of the nightmares to end...

In the tears of the willow there's peace, as calm as the wind blowing over its branches.

Through its leaves, drying its tears brushing them away...

Crowded

Crowded, trapped in a templet of time with no window to excape through. A constant give and pull with nowhere to receive, or restore.

Drained, swirling this continues circle. Trying to balance your feeling with my lack of freedom, constantly being drained, crowded, in the darkness with no privacy, no trust, and watched over, waiting for a mistake, or misleading fact. Crowded in a box with no windows, trapped in a vortex in the cortex of my cerebral, gray matter crashing, shattering slowly into my whirlpool, thats trapped in the constant circle of a drain.

Mistakes

Mistaking my reason for a season, seasons in life is left to not mean anything, with no feeling. Please don't mistake my reason for words not said, please don't mistake my time not spent for time not meant. So much you've missed, so much not mentioned. Do take my love granted when it meant the world to me, i love you is so much more then something that can be measured, in time or one's actions. Remember i didn't let you go for my boat i will row for all of eternity just to be next to you. Don't mistake my reason for a season for my season will never end.

Deadly Passion

When i married her, it was fun, she was new, didn't exactly know what she was getting herself into. But hey it was fun, we were young, and didn't think any of this could come back to haunt us. Innocent. Just kids out having fun. Innocent! What people thought, until the lights went out, with out. Innocent to everyone around us but deep down we knew our inner demons, thats why we were perfect for each other.. She was my better half to my evil, and i was her worshipper!! My goddess leading me straight to the gates of hell, yes I saw it from the beginning, but like every toxic thing not good for you, knowing it will leave you broken, alone or dead, i still wanted her, she was my drug that fed my addition. Dependent on her anger to feed my inner demon, in return kept me faithful. Waiting for night to come so i can be next to her, in her, wild, neck breaking, nail breaking sex that kept me coming back for more.

Sad

Sad. Woke up crying to myself, dry face, dry pillow, but crying. Sad like my heart is breaking from an unknown source, cry from missing an unknown person, crying deep down in my soul as it cracks like a mirror as I stare back at myself, waking up to silence, hot, thirsty, and needing to pee... I don't understand, why am i sad? Why am i falling apart when theres nothing wrong? Why is this silence killing me when it's not even quiet in my room?

Midnight Oil

Feel like burning the midnight oil, tell a story untold, explore all the folds of time and space, trace the lines of time to when time stand still. Where everything works like a mill, constant, blundering, crashing, and thundering. Wondering what comes next according to text, next is the definite in time that cycles in infinity, constantly contouring to the fabric where things live and die, definite in what is true time will always live only question is where will you live in time?

Blank

White, as blank as my essence. As blank as my inner desires. White, the color of my consciousness reflecting in a room with no lights illuminating from the contrast of the still walls. White the color of my canvas before i ruin its perfection with my abstract lines, blacks, blues, and grays placed with no reason other then self expression, and feelings being moved by something wild inside, stroking and stocking underhandedly by and by. The same line twice because you expect perfection but this damn paint brush is anything but. But as i close my eyes and take a deep breath, noticing utter perfection is things that's still, with no movement, essence trapped in time but beauty trapped in it's essence. Like the canvas that i first started on. White

Isolation

You will find peace in isolation. You will find me, in solitude in the darkest pit, losing myself in the darkness surrounding me. Peeling away my flesh, revealing my soul raw, unforgiving, and ready too attack anything that dare step near my isolation, my solitude, my peace. The quietness has consumed me. It's deafening how lonely quietness can be. Forging the mind into a blade, sharp, dark, tuned to be as dissociative as possible in my solitude in the corner off isolation. You can find me in the darkest hole, in the darkest corner of my isolation seeking solitude, peeling away my flesh, eating away at my soul...

Awakening

I feel so alive for so long, hidden away, while trying to maintain an image. I forgot who I was, I forgot how I was, but this is me. The bull that many feared, others hate, is very much alive. Freed from the chain that once held him captive.. ALIVE!! Free to blaze paths, ram what ever gets in it's way, run over and demolish those who try to stop me. Dampened for so long I forgot how good it feels to breath, to feel the blood race through my veins, to lose my self in my temper, I forgot the freedom I fought so long to keep, for what? For who? To fit in? To not be judged by my peers? To please you all and save face to a brighter future? Not anymore, I'm free to run, to speak my mind just because I want to regardless of who watching, who's judging. I refuse to lose my self again to fit in when clearly I was made to stick out and lead. This is who I am and there's no stopping me...

Leave Me To Nothing

So much to say, even more not worth saying, so I sit and yell to myself so no one can hear me. Just me and my thoughts and echoes, of what was and what could have been avoided, oh well leave me to my voices, the yelling, the screaming of my own demise. Leave me to my own universal tools of torture. Leave me to my what have what was, and what is. For this is me and I am it, and it's your worst nightmare. Happy hunting my friends!!

Lost

I need to take a long journey to go and find myself. I don't know where to go right or left to find myself. Not motivated to do anything different, try or explore, can't really say that I want anything more, like I use to want before. Just really want to lay in the floor for a couple of days or more and find a path in my brain to explore in hopes that I'll find the right door that leads me to where I use to be. Fumbling around in a panic, screaming lost again. Damnit!!!!! And it gets worse around the next corner. Mentally escape, that's what I want to do but I can't, damnit!!!! I stepped in some glue, once I break free I'll continue this journey to find the rest of me...

Today's a special day

Today is a special day, it's not only the day I found you but the day that I found myself.

Today's the day you showed me to explore any and all possibilities.

Today's the day you told me it was ok not to just fall for anything and that its ok to have standards.

Today's the day you see that it all paid off as I set the universe upside down as I blaze my own path and take you on a journey to the death of my mind, as you drift to my soul as it caresses your beautiful skin, then onto my heart when it beats and skip a beat to the sound of your voice.

Today's the day I give the world new hope, new paths, new love, new journeys, new possibilities for growth, stimulation, and new visions for the future. Today's your day what are you going to do?

Direction

Heart and mind is awake fully desirable and waiting to take control of my feeling and fate. But wait stand back because you took control that was a huge mistake. To fake, and temp fate with the design of fake temptations thinking it's good for you, here for you, you can't help but follow through. No not today not my faith, you're not going to laugh in my face, grumbling, grabbing, trying to hold on to faith, when you left it behind to chase that behind attached that girl. I showed you the way, I showed you what you could gain if you could only wait. But naaa you had to tempt fate, you couldn't wait, but now it's to late, not looking while your walking was your grave mistake. Now your standing here over your body talking to me as you await my decision. Did you not know I walked with you, guided you, protected you when others meant you harm, don't look down son you're missing an arm, & bleeding out. "oh god save me I'm dying without a doubt." Oh son listen let's take a walk and figure this out.

Knew You

I thought I knew you, from the curve of your smile as it shined brightly through the crowd, I thought I knew you from your soul to your heart because it beats to the same rhythm as mine. I thought I knew you for who you are, the sweet melody of your voice, as your words flow beautifully from your supple lips. I thought I knew you for your truth, trusting blindly as your lies cut deeper and deeper with time. I think I remember you, for any and every time you needed me I was there, the time I swore we were making love it was only a nut for you. I thought I knew you, why do I know you? Why didn't I see you? I thought I saw you deep in your heart, through every emotion, and your ups and downs.. around and around, we go for what reason I'll never know. over the time I let my emotions go losing you hurt unlike any pain you'll ever know. I thought I knew you for who you were but come to find out you had men lined up like a store. this is the end of all i have to write I hope you enjoyed the story I hope you have a good night.

Beautiful Mind

Simple, but yet complex, shades of blues, grays, purples and pinks beautiful, intricate, organized, uniquely divine to its own creation. Beautiful. With each electrical impulse in boding each emotion, action, and feeling. Beautiful mind. Powerful lines of communication from one part of the body to the next, connecting sensation to reality, dreams to fantasies, to see but not see but to understand what have been seen. switching from channel to channel, line to line from left to right, right to left. Beautiful understanding of life and uniquely determining which path to follow, unlike water following the path of least resistance but to resists the path that is selected for you determined to create your own way. Beautiful mind beautiful in thought, beautiful in the way you work.

Troubled Heart

Sometimes I wish we weren't the way we are, sometimes I wish we could have a clean slate for a healthy relationship, sometimes.
If we weren't the way we are now and have been, would I still be the man that I am? Would I still have hurt as many women as I did? Or would I still try as hard to not be like you?
Sometimes I just don't understand how I can have so much love but have so much hatred towards you. I just don't understand.
In one breath we could laugh with each other but the next me trying my best not to disrespect you, so I end up not talking to you for months. Because I would rather not talk to than live knowing that I've disrespected you.
My emotions run wild they are strong, my mind tells me right from

wrong, but my heart says be the fool and give her another chance. Maybe one day but not today I'm not ready not now. These are the troubles of my heart.

Past Impact

So last night my brain did a loop, it wanted me to post something I have already written. Not knowing that it was written in August 2009 but I also knew I was too lazy to rewrite it (lol lazy moment lol) because I knew it was familiar so I went on a hunt (not knowing it would take me back so many years) but going back from who I am now the me that all of my new friends and classmates see and know. Back to who I was, the changes and heartaches, all the time gaps from me deactivating my account, to my son Jeremiah being born and the time I spent with him in my arms and me watching him sleep (because I knew those times was coming to an end) me when I was in church heavy because I didn't know what else to do, all the hatred and anger, me being bitter because of drama with my family, fights with my ex-wife, (god knows her bs should have driven me nuts) past relationships and even when I first started writing. So many emotions bubbled up, so many memories flashed, one thing kept me constant, one thing kept me going. (Fear: fear that I would turn out the way everyone imagined I would be, fear that I would be like everyone that I hated in this world, fear that I would fail myself) the expectation that I would be like my dad, or let my past educational experience affect my future (elementary, middle school, and part of high school 9th and 10 grade I was in ese classes) because I was slower than everyone else, or I was distracted, whatever concept wasn't sticking. But I got through it, I coped with things and started drawing, as I got older I started to write and life because easier, I was able to take control and understand now things stick, (so I guess you can say there was too much on my mind that it was forcing things out). But there's a lot behind that many people don't know, many things untold, and many things and parts of me that people will never see or know. Over the years I've grown, I've changed; I've let go so much (I still have some issues going with my mom and one of my sisters) but idk if those will ever go away. People have said life is what you make it. Yes and no because as a child you have little to no control over your life, as you get older when you're able to make decisions it may not be the right decisions because of the roots from your childhood, or something hindering you from acting freely. Life isn't always what you make it because some people, some religions hinder you from having that choice, freedom. So for those of us that do have that choice make it a good life, make it worth living, make it so you can make an impact on someone else's life...

Canvas

When I'm writing is when I'm at my rawest form, it's also when I'm the most vulnerable. Because I write whatever comes out, no second thoughts, no filters. For these reasons I love writing, it allows me to be free, to be myself without judgement, (because I don't care what anyone else thinks.) whatever comes out here is just there, there's no retracts or maybe I shouldn't have written that... Nope what comes to mind comes out. Writing to me is me and a blank canvas (like art, painting a picture, designing, sketching, or blue printing) it's intimate between me and my canvas at times it's quiet, there's time when there's a deep or phat beat in the back ground, or even just a little love making, baby making music lol you never know like now I'm in the mood for Lincoln Park mixed with a little classical.. Unlike art I can switch scenes without start a new canvas in the middle of a story line. For my readers you can get to know me the true me through my words, lines, and phrases. You can take a walk with me through valleys, to your bedroom making love, to having drinks, or eating fruit. You never know. I like to write to relate to who's reading so. So, they're not just my words, so that they're your words, your fantasy, your path or whatever you may need. So writing isn't just my release it may also be your release because someone understands, have been there, or even freaks your mind the way you never had it done. The canvas is endless the canvas is yours tell me what you want...

Friends

So many friends on Facebook, so many followers on Instagram but not one true friend, someone that I can just chat with, laugh with or just talk about anything with. I guess you can say it's my fault because I'm guarded, or I'll hold my tongue, be quiet, and not try to fully find more things in common with a person for one reason or another. But then there's the other side of no caring to get to know me as well, it's people I could consider as my friends or maybe just people I can have fun with every once in a while.. I can honestly say I thought was my friends when I first started school but after things changed we all changed and apparently went our own directions with out a memo, they just simply stopped answering.. Hints my problem why I'm guarded. (Feels good to write to my self and discover the root of my problems)

Can't Sleep

I can't sleep when I'm all alone, I cant sleep when my heart don't have a song. I can't sleep. I can't sleep when I hear your heart weep, I can't sleep... I can't sleep because the tears won't stop, I cant sleep because my heart don't tick with out your heart tock. I can't sleep. I can't sleep because in my sleep I hear your name, I can't sleep...

DO

Do you see me? Do you see the tears as they escape my souls crying with in, do you see the heartache and see it as it cracks a little more with every beat can you see me?? Can you see my all and all the effort that I put in just to make you happy, to see your smile.. can you see? Can you see deep with in me as I die more and more inside, crying under a rock from missing you? Can you hear? Can you hear the song my heart plays when I'm around you as the violin plays to the sound of your voice.. can you hear can you feel me? Can you feel me and what I feel when I touch you deep in the depths of your soul with every caress? Can you feel me? Can you feel me, late in the night touching you as you moan from missing me, licking you, sucking you, sliding in and out of you? Do you miss the warmth from my side of the bed, my hand on your hip as we sleep the night away? Do you?

IDK

To ask for so much but want so little. To feel like the simplest desire would never be within arm's reach. To have so much love locked away, but burns to get out. To burn with all the passion in the world... the flames from my passion shines so brought that it blocks out the sun, so bright, so strong, but radiant full of life and so many colors, full of love, passion and an undeniable urge for success...

Sleepless Nights

Lonely, burning desirer to do more, mind is like a radio station booming 24hours a day, awake to every lasting thought, memories running like the interstate to fast to keep up with, to much to focus on one thing.

Sleepless nights where your body is ready to go to sleep, but your mind won't let you, because it's so much more you want to know or want to do. May even be because your body is so use to running it forgot how to rest. Sleepless nights, where you miss a certain someone, your mind/body won't let you stop thinking about his or her last touch, kiss, and even the last words they spoke. Sleepless nights happen to all of us, some for other reasons. If you would like to share a sleepless night with me, feel free to leave a comment, a little feedback would be nice...

Under Construction

Up on the edge of my bed thinking about the quickest way to die with out any having to clean up behind me, nor freaking out when they find me, thinking to leave a note or not, na no note i write enough i been writing for so long about so many things every one that know me know every thing about me so no more words. No good byes, I think the world would be better off with out me and every one can move on as if i never was here. So many ways to die but every death have a different meaning so i'll make up one of my own do something i can do with out freaking any one out, don't worry it wont be any cutting, or meds, or me drinking any thing..There will be no hanging or waiting to be found. So just do something my body do on it's own just got to remind my self not to come out of it nor to wake up. So i guess this is my own little way of being me leave to make everyone else happy so oh well not like i did right by anyone in my life any way. Bye bye for now see you on the other side...

Guilty

I'm guilty of not being enough.
Guilty of not doing enough..
I'm guilty of being selfish in what I want.
I'm guilty in not compromising in my selfishness..

I'm guilty and I'm sorry...

Sorry for letting you down, not being what you need from me...

I'm sorry that I haven't been able to be there to protect you...

Sorry that I fall short.

I'm sorry that my love comes with heartache, discomfort and the forever thought of when he's going to get tired and walk away.

I'm sorry that I made you love me and I haven't kept up my end of the bargain..

No Space

There is no calm

There isn't enough space

There's nowhere to project my energy, there's no space

The once calm, that I once known is nowhere to be found and all I want, that I long for is a piece of solace in a world filled with chaos.

There's no room

there's no room to breathe with the ever-changing wall closes in closer and closer

There's no space

There's no space, no escape, no corner of my own to turn to, there's no quietness to turn to, there's no out, with no out, turn in

Within yourself to fine peace, solace, the calm you once knew, and to escape the chaos. Turn in to find a way out

In the rain

I remember when I lived in Florida and on those rainy days I would go out and sit on my picnic table (yes I really had one in my front yard) but I would go out and sit, let all my worries fade away, feeling like nothing else in the world mattered, just me in the rain, those days were the days of cleansing, open every window I could find, open my door and let the wind rush through. For that day I would escape the world that I knew, no phone calls, no television, no visitors. It was my day to clean, rearrange, and sit in a corner and cry (if needed). Rain for me have always been my very own reset button, cleansing for my soul, the peace in the middle of a storm, the focus of releasing my pain.. In the rain I found peace, clarity, understanding, and my beginning to a better day..

Chapter 6
Twisted
Tapping

There's a tapping on the wall!! Come here put your ear to it, I'm waiting!! Yea that's it come closer, yea a little more. That's it give me your head, yea that's it. Say hello to my blade as it slams through your skull entertaining me as I release. As I watch you lose consciousness, as your blood run down your face, filling the room with the smell of death, ejaculating over your dying face from the smell of fresh blood driving we up the wall. Ahhh I can live in this moment forever, now to the tub to drain you for a warm bath. I've told you before every action comes with consequences, but noooo you didn't hear me, now you're learning. Funny how your vision plays tricks on the mind as you're dying, how your hearing dampen. Oh, I know how you feel, I've been there, over-dosed 3 times!!! THREE and I'm still here!! I've split my throat, the veins in my wrists more times than I can remember!!! AND STILL STUCK HERE!!! In this fucking hell hole of a life.. But I guess I was saved to teach you this lesson hahaha!!! This is so fulfilling feeling your hot blood flowing over me slowly as gravity does its job. Ohh yea the smell of you over me turns me on so much!! I just want to take you down and skull fuck you until you take your last breath. But you would enjoy it to much I'll wait until you can't benefit from my pleasure!!!

Dead

3.)Im dead because you killed me, slowly, time after time, growing weaker and weaker as time ticks away. Listening to my heart pound in my ears as the blood escape my body growing weaker by the second. the same heart you took for granted the Times you stared into my eyes and seen my heart for what it was, second guessed in a blink of an eye. I'm dead because you killed me!! 2.) Nothing has never been sweeter then the first cut. the cut that disconnected me from my soul setting it free like a bird free from the aches of life. I'm dead, sitting here in the tub soaking think-ing about what happened, what could've happened and what could've been repeating "there were no love greater lost then found" carving it up my arms. I feel nothing once and forever broken, nothing desired, nothing felt, nothing to gain and nothing to lose. as the blades dig deeper into my flesh laughing deliciously to the treat of pain...

1.) Death. sitting in the dark staring out in space, looking death in the eye. I fear you not and I welcome humbly no love lost no love found repeats in my head, wondering why? Why live, why fight to survive, why should I or anyone else care. as my moral logical mind began to escape me. Close your eyes and listen to me, I'll show you the way out.

Get the riddle? No? Read it again but this time follow the numbers in order.

Love Affair

In times of darkness the truth will bring you light. If you seek the light seek the one who provides it for you to see..

"Come in, and close the door, cut off your phone.. Get undressed, come here" she said "I've been waiting on you" "wait" he said "what about your husband?" "Oh I'm working late" she said "yea you are working late he" replied as they laughed, as he asked her "why, why cheat, do he not treat you right?" "No she replied I'm happy he treat me like a queen, I just want you.." "Mmmm" he said, as she got on her knees, as she slurp on his dick taking it deeper and deeper as he leaned his head back, as he asked her "Are you sure you want to do this?" as she replied "ssshhh come give me that dick!!" Pulling him down on top of her. As he entered her slowly, striking over and over as she screamed with delight.. As I walked through the house, past the kitchen, down the hall to the gun case. I reached for my 9 & two clips, the shot gun she brought me with the engravement LOVE FOREVER clinching it tighter and tighter as I loaded each slug.. As I chocked it he stopped and said "shh!! what was that?" as he listened, she said "nothing" as she turned over for him as he slid his dick back in her from the back. Doggy style as she likes it. I closed my eyes not thinking clearly. Thinking about the moments we shared, as I made my way up stairs, down the hall cutting through the bathroom entering the room and pressed the end of my cold steel barrel against his bold head, as he went limp she turned to look back at him she faced the barrel of my 9... Damn.... As I repeated the questions, ... calmly, from before they started.... Demanding an answer, as he went to answer he felt a nudge from the shot gun, "not you" I said "her"!!! In shock the words fumbled from her mouth "I... I..... I thought you were on a business trip"... "Answer me!!!" I said "Why?" "Why not just leave?" As the years rolled down her face, she yelled I don't know. Don't lie to me moving my finger closer to the trigger narrowing down my aim.. Wait yelled the guy, glancing down at him I asked "what?" He mumbled I asked the same thing. But it didn't stop you.. As I slammed him in the head with the butt of the shot gun as he fail over she went to catch him don't move I yelled.. Why I asked holstering my 9.. now facing my shot gun.. Why, she explained that she have been seeing him for years. As I started to squeeze the trigger.... Buzz buzz buzz my alarm goes off... Lol ahh just a dream..

Vampire Kisses

Ssshhhh! You hear that? Listen...... Do you hear? Whispering in your ear, the calling of someone calling your name? Mmmmm come here, look so tasty. Come to me, join me... Closer... Closer... Don't resist let me kiss you as i hold you close, sinking my teeth into your neck, tasting you with my vampier kisses. Mmmmm you can't resist as you look at me from across the room, smelling my sweet scent as it linger across the room, so you speak as i smile, and politely excuse myself to the bed room as you follow closely, high off of the passion as it rise with every stop, teasing you with my forbidden scent, into the room we go as i lay you on the bed, striping your clothes off, paralyzed from my poisonous kisses as i work my way down your body, pass your breast, your tummy, sinking my teeth into your inner thigh, pleasing you with the forbidden poison as i turn you into one of my kind, my flesh of your flesh, together forever...... Come here let me taste you with my vampire kisses, come here, closer...... Closer.......

5am

It's five in the morning and I'm wide awake. It's when I wake up when I'm not working, it's when I start to get sleepy when I'm at work. It's when I'm more motivated to write, it's when riddles and rhymes bounce around, as dj's to rhythms screams out instructions to jump around. Letters like quakes slam the ground, bouncing sentence structures all around, making a unique sound, make structures and quick phrases like man, I ain't fooling around!! Jumbled up, then knocked down by a killer fresh clown, spitting lines and with lyrics that makes your skin tingle when you hear it! Talking about bars you never know how far he might go, like I said he have killer flo! You know, like knocking on your door, while standing by the shore a 100miles away, that mind is sharp, just thinking about it his rhymes gets you excited like you just killed a shark.. But it's 5am I'm wide awake, it's when music quake in my mind, reminding me it's time to get up and grind, or while I'm at work it's almost bed time.. It's five in the morning, what are you doing?

Who Am I

I'm your lover your best friend, I'm the one that please you every night, I'm that freak in the sheets that smacks your ass and pull your hair while deep inside you, I'm the reasons for your orgasms... who am I? Demetri, I'm the flirt, I'm the one who chase for the love of the game, I'm the one that if you get wrong, he cut loose the bull, I'm the one that can act as bullish as I need to be and not give a fuck!! Who am I? Omar, I'm the who you ask for help, the one that can be anything you could ever want, I'm the one that can fix your phone, computer, table, chairs, the one that can fix anything his hands touches, I'm the one who can answer any odd ball off the wall question that 9 out of 10 people can't answer who am I? Deshane, I'm the one that will tell you about your ass and not give a fuck what comes out or how it comes out, I'm the one who will never back down from a challenge or fight, I'm the one that would hurt you and stand over you and smile while your laying there crying, im the one who you would see last while you're lingering with in the last inches of your life, I'm the one who know the human body as well as I know my hand, every fiber of my being, and how much energy it takes to disable a limb or body.. What's my last name? Barnes

I'm the best person you could ever meet, the one who would give you his last the one that would give the shirt off of his back, the one who would give up his jacket in the freezing cold so you could be warm!!!

I'm the last person you would ever want to lose, the last person you would ever want to walk away from, and the last person you would ever want a problem with... Who am I??

Antisocial

I don't want to smile.. Don't feel like greeting you. No I can't give you directions. No I don't know what floor you want to go to nor do I care. Oohh you want keys? What keys? There's no keys at this desk.. No I don't want your keys nor your radio, take it with you bring them back in the morning. Write my report? Oh no I'll pass, how bout I give you a run down of events and you write it!! No I don't want to lock up, I don't want to patrol, how bout I sit here and look pretty and you patrol.. I want to go home cut on my xbox and shoot people and things until my eyes hurt as I let my skin breath.. Laughing at you foolish person for not having your access card to get in and out of the parking garage.. No I can't well won't let you out, access denied!! Comeback through the lobby and call a cab your car will be here when you return with your card!!

What's in the closet?

What's in the closet? The fears of others, as I was the last thing they saw. The demon in the night from all of the blood stains washed from the clothes.

What's in the closet? The memories and energy that attached to me, as they would not be forgotten.

What's in the closet? The weight of the world, all the tears from all the lost souls, all the wombs, cuts, pain, and memories of healing.

What's in the closet? The last body of my enemy, myself, peaking out at me, waiting for the moment to get free in the darkness. So, I close that door every night and lock it to ensure that he stay in place, never to taste the freedom of darkness.

what's in the closet? My secrets, my past, the toll I'll have to answer for at the end..

Box Of Shadows

There's a leak in my box of shadows, that's locked away inside of my closet. Inside this box live the horror of what is and what was! The screams, deaths, and countless tears live in that box, the six-year-old me that only wants his mom that he once knew and cried for. My shadow of horror lives there forever waiting for a moment to escape and run free in this peaceful world that I created, that once belonged to a life of wrong-doing in order to survive. This box of shadows is home to every horror in the world, the forsaken of peace, and all the horrors that will keep anyone awake.

There's a leak in my box of shadows and last night my shadow got free. It ran loose and caused as much havoc as can be. The once peaceful world was on fire, the box of horror was destroyed, and now I must go hunt. Hunting in the darkness of what is my mind, the forest lies and disruption, is nauseating, trying, and I must muster through. Face the deception, the hard times, the flames and expose my bare bones, but I must muster through, I must March on, and make it through. I must find all who play and dance here, they must be locked away.

Renegade

The first time I laid eyes on him was off 59th Avenue, after a drug bust in a major warehouse. He watched from the back of his Lincoln, parked 5 yards from the fence line, puffing on a cigar with a condescending smile on his face.

I was once a happy cop. I survived 4 world tours on a specialized team. After 5 years I decided to get out and live a normal life. I had an amazing wife that I met when I was in the Core. We lived an ideal life together.

I've been on the police force for 15 years now. All was well until I ran across a known drug ring out of Mexico. The leader's name is Frost. Very few people have seen his face. He bought his property from a corrupt politician that has a "secret" account in the Cayman Islands.

I remember waking up to the sun, glistening through the blinds. Shining against your skin as it glows with warmth as you lay in my arms with your head on my chest. I slowly run my fingertip up and down your spine, lightly, careful not to wake you. As I lay here on my back, I think about the previous day, where it all starts.

It's a typical, early Saturday morning. I step out of the shower and start to make my normal early morning phone calls. As usual, my partner calls to fill me in on what supplies have been moved from one warehouse to another. I get dressed and load up my truck. As I pull out to f the driveway, I see you passing. I think nothing of it as I continue to pull out of my driveway.

As the day goes on, I have completed 5 deliveries. I head to Jimmy John's for my favorite sandwich. As I sit down to eat I receive a text message saying "How's your day going daddy?" I responded "Good, by the way who is this?" As I take the first bite of my sandwich I think "Uhh, wrong number".

As I finish my lunch my alarm goes off reminding me, I have a meeting in 45 minutes. I pack up my trash and throw it away. As I start out the door, I hear "Sir, you forgot your key." and he walks over to hand them to me. I look down and see my keys in my hand. I smile and say" Sorry, I have my keys right here". As I look up at the keys in his hand, I notice something familiar about the key. This is the key I had made for her. I take the key as a tear runs down my face.

I get back in my truck and put the key in my cup holder. I sit and stare in the rear view mirror as memories come flashing back to me. I am quickly interrupted by a text saying "You'll find out tonight". I convince myself it is still the wrong number and don't think anything of it. Onto my meeting.

When the meeting is over, I head home. Pulling into the garage I notice a single rose petal with shades of white and pink. As I round my truck an alarm goes off in my head. I don't have a rose bush, nor do my neighbors. Standing at the end of the driveway, with the petal in my hand, I notice an approaching car. I think of how strange this day is becoming. The wind blows as I raise my hand and let the petal float away in the breeze.

I unlock the door and walk into the house. I walk into my bedroom, turn the shower on and get undressed. I step in and think about the last time I saw you. Think about how you smiled at me and walked out of my life, taking that new job offer. Getting out of the shower I dry off, thinking about what I should wear tonight.........it's a nice night for black, I think to myself.

I pull up to the bar. There is music blasting as I walk in. I shake hands with security as everyone greets me. One face sticks out of the crowd more than the others. I look into her eyes. As she gets closer I can smell the sweet smell of her perfume. Time stops and the music dampens.

Flashbacks start to play in my head. I remember your soft skin and the feel of your lips. I pull you from the bar stool, holding you in my arms with a warm embrace. We whisper "I missed you so much" in each other's ears.

We leave the bar and head to the beach. Hand in hand we walk under the night sky together, for hours. Who knows how much time has passed by? As the night gets late we head to my place. I think "Oh my God, I can't wait". We pull into the driveway and I open your door, remembering the last time your clothes hit my floor. As time ticks on you lay closer to me, resting your head on my chest. I kiss your forehead and tell you "I love you". Holding you through the night, wishing this moment would never end. The sun is rising, glistening through the blinds, shining against your skin as it glows with warmth. You lay in my arms with your head on my chest, as I slowly run my fingertip up and down your spine. Ever so gently so as not to wake you.

As I lay here on my back, I think back over that night. Where it starts and how it ended. A love so deep came to an end. I lost my lover and my best friend. In the end, you came home to rest until our souls meet again.

Years later, I ran into an old friend. We talked with each other for months. Then we got married, my life was whole again. I returned to work. Frost fell off the map, no longer a threat. Things were returning to normal.

Well, at least, I thought so.....

Chapter 2 Collision

Five hours into my shift I walk into my office and notice a package. It reads "open me if you dare". Calling my partner and chief into my office, we opened the package to find a DVD. I set the DVD to play. What we saw that day was enough to set any man over the edge. Realizing, in order to beat Frost, there couldn't be any rules. No limitations. I have to become a Renegade.

So, now I'm dead. Dead because YOU killed me. After a lifetime of friendship, I am forced to live without you. I am a Renegade after my own heart. Speeding, crazy off of Red Bulls, vodka and 5 hour energy mixes. Trying to go faster and faster. My heart pumps faster and harder. I'm sweating with chills and tingling everywhere!!!!! Driving fast, speeding, gripping the wheel. Going a buck fifty, bobbing and weaving through traffic as my music blares in my ears. Not a care in the world, just me in the moment. Quick, sharp turns as I drift all my problems away. The rubber meets the road and the smoke smacks the ass of my car. Oh, it feels so good! As I hit the corner at 4 G's, ssshhh, listen to the engine purr as the pedal meets the floor. As I go faster and faster, past the point of no return. Hold on tight, if I fuck up now it's all over! Do I back off now, or push a little harder and get it all in? Major question, one simple answer. Fuck it, let's go! It's all or nothing.

Drunk in a world full of blood hungry vampires, searching for the one who took your heart. I'm a rabble flipping table. Shoot first, ask questions later. The last thing I remember you saying is "don't worry about me." Leaving nothing more than tears and sorrow.

As day turns to night, I see you over and over in my mind. Twisting and turning with every thought. As each day passes, I get closer to the man that took you from me. Plans of torture play over and over in my mind. As each day passes, I want to kill more and more.